CW00538078

LOVE &
ROMANCE
FACTS, FIGURES & FUN

*"Any book without a mistake in it has had
too much money spent on it"*

Sir William Collins, publisher

LOVE &
ROMANCE

FACTS, FIGURES & FUN

EVE DEVEREUX

For P.D.S. – who else?

Love & Romance
Facts, Figures & Fun

Published by
Facts, Figures & Fun, an imprint of
AAPPL Artists' and Photographers' Press Ltd.
10 Hillside, London SW19 4NH, UK
info@ffnf.co.uk   www.ffnf.co.uk
info@aappl.com   www.aappl.com

Sales and Distribution
UK and export: Turnaround Publisher Services Ltd.
orders@turnaround-uk.com
USA and Canada: Sterling Publishing Inc. sales@sterlingpub.com
Australia & New Zealand: Peribo Pty. peribomec@bigpond.com
South Africa: Trinity Books. trinity@iafrica.com

A catalogue record for this book is available from the
British Library.

ISBN 1 904332 331

Design (contents and cover): Malcolm Couch
mal.couch@blueyonder.co.uk

Printed in China by Imago Publishing
info@imago.co.uk

Contents

WHAT IS THIS THING CALLED LOVE?

Through the centuries, many have attempted, with greater or lesser success, to tie down exactly what it is that love is.

By contrast, some languages, such as Papuan, do not have a word for love at all.

Ambrose Bierce, in his *The Devil's Dictionary* (1906), was succinct on the subject:

Love, n. A temporary insanity curable by marriage or by removal of the patient from the influences under which he incurred the disorder. This disease, like *caries* and many other ailments, is prevalent only among civilized races living under artificial conditions; barbarous nations breathing pure air and eating simple food enjoy immunity from its ravages. It is sometimes fatal, but more frequently to the physician than to the patient.

Because of the imprecision of the definition of the word "love", and because the emotion itself is so unsusceptible to rational analysis, philosophers have had a millennia-long field-day on the subject. One approach has been to break love down into three constituent aspects: *eros, philia* and *agape*.

Eros is intense, passionate desire, not necessarily sexual though perhaps best exemplified by sexual desire. According to Plato, *eros* is the desire for a transcendental beauty which we can never perceive until we die but of which we are constantly "reminded" by the beauties we perceive in the world around us. Our love is thus not for a particular person or object but for the elements they possess of the unique, universal, transcendent beauty. Love is therefore rational and objective at root, and its experience a distinction between man and the animals; irrational desire, as in the physical expression of love, is of a lower order, being shared by the beasts of forest and field.

Philia incorporates such tamer emotions as friendship, affection and loyalty. Aristotle devoted much of his *Nicomachean Ethics* to the topic of *philia*, and distinguished between the philia derived from self-interest and that derived from particularized philanthropy – which distinction, he further suggested, might disappear in such instances as secretly doing someone a good turn because of the personal pleasure one gains in so doing. Like Plato on *eros*, Aristotle was keen to present *philia* as fundamentally rational: one does not feel it toward those who are undeserving of it, while one is most likely to feel it intensely toward those of similar disposition to oneself. The perfect *philia* would be experienced between people who were rational and profoundly happy. A precondition for being able to feel *philia* toward others is to feel it toward oneself.

Agape is epitomized in the love felt for humankind by God and by humankind for God, but the concept is broader than that, extending to include the love one can feel for all humanity. In this sense it draws upon both *eros* and *philia*, in that it is ideal – it is a love that sees past the reality to the transcendent, and it does not require love to be returned – while also being a profound form of affection or friendship.

The early Christian writers were especially keen on *agape*. (In the early Church the word had another important meaning, as "love feast".) They pointed to passages in the Old Testament concerning the need to love God entirely and also to "love thy neighbour as thyself". Christ, according to the gospels, extended this also to loving "thine enemies"– a dictum that has thrown philosophers of all varieties, not just Christian, into some ethical difficulty: Is it ethically viable to love a neighbour who manifestly does not deserve such love? Is turning the other cheek to bullies and tyrants the correct ethical course? Such questions haven't really been resolved. One Platoesque compromise is to regard love for all humanity as being love for the *ideal* of humanity – for the soul, if you like – while being a bit less than 100% loving toward certain particular individuals.

Aristotle, in *Nicomachean Ethics*, was also concerned that a universal *philia* – in other words, *agape* – necessarily resulted in a dilution. We feel more *philia* toward relatives and those close to us than we do toward distant acquaintances (and, obviously, people we've never met). He summed up thus: "One cannot feel *philia* to a multitude of people in the sense of having *philia* of the perfect type with them, just as one cannot experience *eros* [be in love with] many people at once, for *eros* is a sort of excess of feeling, and it is the nature of such to be felt only toward one person." Such love he described as being a matter of one soul in two bodies.

From the Platonic ideal of love emerged, in Europe from about the 12th century onwards, the concept of courtly or romantic love, as supposedly experienced between knights and damsels and as expressed through the songs of the troubadours. The characteristics of courtly love were: it should be experienced at a physical and/or social distance; the woman was in a dominant and the man in a subservient position within the essentially nonexistent relationship;

the unattainability of the woman (very often the target of all the yearnings was already married, and to a man of high position); and a lack of physical consummation despite endless speculation by the male as to the ecstasies such consummation would hold.

In fact, the term "courtly love" was not coined (as *amour courtois*) until 1883, by Gaston Paris, so it has been suggested there was never any such thing. However, synonyms such as *fine amour* and *vrai amour* were in existence much earlier – and of course there were the troubadour songs, the recountings of chivalric legends, and so on. The *ideal* of courtly love was a fact, even if its real-life manifestation was at best rare, and came to prominence at the court of Eleanor of Acquitaine, Queen of France and subsequently of England, in the 12th century.

The concept of courtly or romantic love in turn exerted an influence on the Romantic movement, which began in the late 18th century in Western Europe and cannot really be said ever to have ended. Linguistically, French and the other Latin and Greek-derived languages are known as "Romance" as opposed to "Germanic" languages. The word "romance" in medieval France was used to describe poems and tales written in the vernacular French rather than the official Latin. Over time it came to be used to describe the subject matter of the poetry written in the vernacular, which tended to be those subjects which we now look upon as "romantic". "Romanticism" has no clear definition, but was in part a 19th-century revolt against the Enlightenment, with Feeling becoming considered to be as important as Reason, in part a rebellion against the old social structures – such as the aristocracy – in part a somewhat overflowered dragging of Nature and her mysterious wonders back into centre stage, in part the celebration of a Golden Age That Never Was, and in part a reassertion of the romantic ideals expressed in the legends of such chivalric heroes as Charlemagne, Sigurd, Alexander the Great and especially King Arthur and the Knights of the Round Table.

In this latter context the tale of Tristan and Isolde was perfectly tailored for the Romantic movement since it in effect had things both ways: a courtly love which could never be consummated between the two principals but which was nevertheless consummated . . . through no fault of the principals, whose virtue could remain intact because they were acting under the irresistible influence of a love philtre.

Among those composers whose works can be considered in whole or in part as belonging to the mainstream of the Romantic movement are Barber, Beethoven, Berlioz, Bizet, Chopin, Grieg, Liszt, Mahler, Moussorgsky, Rimski-Korsakov, Schubert, Schumann, Sibelius, Richard Strauss, Tchaikovsky, Vaughan Williams, Verdi, Weber and Wagner – Wagner most particularly, because his life's work was rooted in Teutonic myth and legend.

Among artists associated with the Romantic movement are Blake, Constable, Delacroix, Caspar David Friedrich, Géricault, Goya, Palmer, the Pre-Raphaelites, Tiedeman and Turner.

Writers especially associated with the Romantic movement include Honoré de Balzac, William Blake, the Brontë sisters, Lord Byron, Samuel Taylor Coleridge, James Fenimore Cooper, Emily Dickinson, Alexandre Dumas, Ralph Waldo Emerson, Théophile Gautier, Johann Wolfgang von Goethe, the Brothers Grimm, Nathaniel Hawthorne, Victor Hugo, Washington Irving, John Keats, Charles Lamb, Mikhail Lermontov, Henry Wadsworth Longfellow, James Macpherson ("Ossian"), Herman Melville, Adam Mickiewicz, Edgar Allan Poe, Alexandr Pushkin, Friedrich von Schiller, Sir Walter Scott, Mary Shelley, Percy Bysshe Shelley, Robert Southey, Stendhal, Henry David Thoreau, Walt Whitman, John Greenleaf Whittier, William Wordsworth and William Butler Yeats.

The reclamation by the Romanticists of their national legendary heritage led often to a cultural nationalism that was not in itself a bad thing but could all too easily degenerate into a base political nationalism – *eros* and *agape* becoming a perverted form of *philia* – and this tended to tar the Romantic movement as a whole. The composers Richard Wagner and Richard Strauss were two who followed this fell path. In the modern era of global communications the danger has lessened: the tales of King Arthur are no longer part of just England's heritage so much as part of *world* heritage, which is what they really were in the first place.

————————

"The most powerful symptom of love is a tenderness which becomes at times almost unbearable."
Victor Hugo

"Love sought is good, but given unsought is better."
William Shakespeare

COURTSHIP
AND LOVEPLAY

KISSING

On average, each of us spends a total of about two weeks of our lives engaged in kissing.

The record for the longest single, continuous kiss currently stands at over 30 hours; obviously such "endurance kisses" are done purely as stunts. Not all lengthy kisses, however, are perpetrated for such reasons: the Maraichins, a people of Brittany, pioneered a practice known as *maraichinage*, a likely precursor of the French kiss in which the two partners, sometimes over a period of several hours, carried out a comprehensive tongued investigation of the interior of each other's mouths.

KISSING IN HISTORY

Although we might consider kissing instinctive, in fact its introduction as part of romantic behaviour seems to date from relatively recently in human history – while of course even in some cultures today the habit has yet to catch on: many of the Eskimo peoples still rub noses where the rest of us might kiss.

The origins of mouth-to-mouth kissing may lie in the primate practice of a mother transferring food directly from her own mouth to her baby's. In time the action of touching lips, with or without food, became a gesture of affection.

Straightforward kissing of the face or other parts of the body seems descended from the general primate behaviour of grooming; kissing is widely observed among the primates.

Another explanation for mouth-to-mouth kissing is that our prehistoric forebears sniffed each others' faces when they met, originally warily but in time as a greeting, and that the touching of lips to cheeks, and finally of lips to lips, developed from there.

A further notion is that prehistoric people believed, as many in less developed cultures do today, that breath carried the essence of the soul. By kissing, therefore, two people were exchanging something very precious to them. Of course, it is equally possible that things were the other way round, that the belief in the nature of the breath emerged from the pre-existing practice of kissing.

Before mouth-to-mouth kissing caught on as a general expression of love, or as part of foreplay, kissing of the hands or feet was employed ceremonially as a sign of respect, authority, friendship, admiration and the like. The Roman Emperors allowed the kissing of themselves by others to act as a sort of public ratings scale of importance: most were confined to kissing the emperor's feet; luckier dignitaries might kiss his hands; and the most important of all could kiss his cheek.

The first Western country in which mouth-to-mouth romantic kissing really caught on appears to have been France, where, in the 6th century, formal dancers would conclude each dance by exchanging a kiss. From this limited usage spread the idea of kissing as a demonstration of affection and intimacy. The Russians copied the notion from the French; and it was in Russia that the exchange of a kiss was first added to the wedding ceremony.

The kissing by adult males of each other's cheeks as a sign of friendship or affection is widespread except in those countries whose cultures are predominantly white Anglo-Saxon – where even hugging between males can be frowned upon.

In 1564 the government of Naples tried to outlaw kissing as a repulsive practice. Kissing in public could incur a hefty prison sentence, up to life; while public kissing within sight of an authority figure could bring the death penalty.

In an old English custom, women would go to country fairs bearing a clove-studded apple (long regarded as an erotic fruit, as evidenced by the assumption, unsupported in *Genesis*, that it was an apple Eve plucked in the Garden of Eden). Whenever she saw a man she'd like to kiss, she would hold the apple to his mouth so that he could chew a clove and then kiss her. The cloves had the effect of freshening the breath in an age long before anyone had much idea of oral hygiene.

The *Ananga Ranga*, an ancient love manual, suggests that couples make a practice of kissing whenever they're in the full flight of argument with each other. In this way, the book proposes, they will forget what they were arguing about and be restored to harmony.

Recent scientific research shows that almost all of the facial muscles – up to 34 – are used in the act of enthusiastic kissing. Psychologists have suggested that kissing may also be a useful relaxation technique, in that the muscular conformation is

HEALTH BENEFITS

Kissing is good for the teeth and gums. It stimulates saliva flow, thereby reducing plaque levels.

Kissing helps you lose weight. It's impossible to put a figure to the exact number of calories you burn with a kiss, because there are so many variables involved, but it may be as high as several calories per minute. In order to achieve significant weight-loss you'd have to kiss very often and for very extended periods — another incentive.

Like many forms of exercise — especially "risk" sports like bungee-jumping — kissing stimulates the production in the brain of the neurotransmitters dopamine, norepinephrine and phenylethylamine. These are chemicals similar to those in amphetamine drugs, and their effect is much the same, only better: they attach to the brain's pleasure receptors to generate moods of euphoria and elation.

As with amphetamine drugs, and for the same reason, some people are susceptible to becoming addicted to kissing: the pleasure receptors involved set up a constant demand for "repeat performances". In the case of kissing, this is usually of little importance; but a similar addiction to sex can be almost as destructive to lives and relationships as substance abuse. Such organizations as SLAA (Sex & Love Addicts Anonymous) are available for help in such cases.

very similar to that of a smile, and the act of smiling usually improves the mood.

Further scientific research, done by Oner Güntürkün and published in Nature in February 2003, has observed how kissing couples generally turn their heads while kissing so as to avoid their noses getting in the way. According to Güntürkün's observations, the mutual tilting of the head is to the right (clockwise) about twice as often as it is to the left. This could be to do with handedness or it could be behaviour learned immediately following birth, when the newborn display a similar ratio of preference for the right over the left.

French kissing appears to have nothing specific to do with France; it's something of a mystery as to how the term originated. The French themselves call such kissing *rouler une pelle* ("to roll a shovel"). Until recently, French kissing was relatively unknown in the East, but the practice has become increasingly prevalent there, presumably due to the influence of Hollywood.

———— UNDER THE MISTLETOE ————

There are various explanations of the origin of the tradition whereby lovers and wannabe lovers kiss under the mistletoe. In one, it is claimed that the Druids believed the plant's berries were the seed of the gods: if squeezed, the berries seep a semen-like liquid. The plant accordingly had aphrodisiac qualities bequeathed from on high. Our modern kiss under the mistletoe is presumably, then, a cleaned-up version of the Druidic tradition.

Whatever one thinks of the Druidic legend, the mistletoe has a long tradition as a healing plant – it is one of several plants to have received the colloquial name All-Heal. A kiss under the mistletoe might thus have been seen as a guarantor of good health to the parties involved, and their union.

In Norse mythology, the god Balder – son of Frigga – was treacherously killed using an arrow made from a bough of mistletoe. The white berries of mistletoe were Frigga's tears at the loss of her son; she cursed the plant for ever more. In some versions of the tale, Frigga was so delighted when Balder was restored to life that she removed the stigma from the plant and promised to kiss anyone passing under it.

According to legend, the mistletoe was a plant of truce during the Middle Ages: enemies who came across it together had to give up their fight until the following day. Thus hanging mistletoe in the home ensured domestic harmony, and people kissed under it as a further sign of goodwill.

Because of the Druidic – i.e., pagan – connection, many early Christians banned mistletoe from their homes. There thus came into being, associated with Christmas, the tradition of the "kissing bough", which was a garland, decorated festively, that hung from the ceiling and under which people kissed. In due course the kissing bough became generally referred to as the mistletoe, even though it wasn't.

"I have found men who didn't know how to kiss.
I've always found time to teach them."
Mae West

———— KISSING IN THE MOVIES ————

The first cinema kiss occurred in 1896 in a movie short, *The Kiss* – a filming of the final scene in a stage musical called *The Widow Jones.* The kissers were John C. Rice and May Irwin. Their 15-second kiss brought the first demands for movie censorship.

For many years the record for the longest screen kiss in a commercial feature movie was held by *You're In the Army Now* (1941), the kissers being the movie's two stars, Jane Wyman and Regis Toomey. It lasted 185 seconds. In 2004 that record was broken by Poonam Daryanani and Sohaib Illyasi, who sustained a kiss for over four minutes in the Indian movie *Mamyab Raste.* The record is particularly notable since until 1978 kissing was banned from Indian movies altogether. All such efforts are dwarfed, however, by the Andy Warhol movie *Kiss* (1963), in which the screen is filled for the movie's entire 50-minute running time by kisses, each lasting something over three minutes. The kissing between Naomi Levine and Rufus Collins was sufficiently popular that the cinematic short *Naomi and Rufus Kiss* was released the following year.

Another celebrated long screen kiss is that in Norman Jewison's *The Thomas Crown Affair* (1968) between Steve McQueen and Faye Dunaway. Although it lasts only about a minute, it took a total, spread across several days, of over eight hours to film.

♡

The record for the most kisses performed by an actor in a movie is held by John Barrymore, who, dividing his attentions between Mary Astor and Estelle Taylor, delivered no fewer than 191 kisses during the 127 minutes of Alan Crosland's 1926 epic *Don Juan.*

There are plenty of kisses between various couples in Tony Larder's 1997 movie *Unspoken*. The sound effects for all of these kisses were separately recorded by Larder, kissing his own hands.

The theatrical trailer for *The Adventures of Robin Hood* (1938) shows Robin (Errol Flynn) and Maid Marian (Olivia de Havilland) kissing. Moviegoers were doomed to disappointment: the kiss belonged to a scene that was deleted before the movie's release.

Generally reckoned the best kiss in the cinema is that between Ingrid Bergman and Cary Grant in Alfred Hitchcock's *Notorious* (1946). The kissing between Sigourney Weaver and Mel Gibson in *The Year of Living Dangerously* (1982) is consciously modelled upon it – director Peter Weir insisted the two stars watch the scene over and over until they could do it right themselves. In fact, the kiss in *Notorious* is really a series of short kisses, the two stars separating momentarily betweentimes. The regulations currently in force restricted on-screen kisses to just a couple of seconds; Hitchcock was intent on making nonsense of the rule.

Another front-runner for best on-screen kissing is that between Vivien Leigh and Clark Gable in *Gone With the Wind* (1939). Later Leigh is claimed to have said she disliked performing the part because of Gable's halitosis.

In David Lean's 1965 movie *Doctor Zhivago*, the first kiss between Victor Komarovsky (Rod Steiger) and Lara Antipova (Julie Christie) has been much remarked upon for Christie's portrayal of startled resistance. Her reactions were genuine: Steiger deliberately surprised her by sticking his tongue into her mouth. Also genuinely surprised was actor Matthew McConaughey in 2003's *How to Lose a Guy in 10 Days* when Kate Hudson suddenly planted kisses all over his face. The kissing was a spur-of-the-moment improvisation by Hudson.

John Wayne inflicted an unexpected professional injury in John Ford's *The Quiet Man* (1952). In the scene where he first kisses Maureen O'Hara, the script called for her to slap his face. In blocking her blow he broke a bone in her hand.

British audiences for the 1930 movie *The Flame of Love* (a.k.a. *Road to Dishonour*) saw nothing unusual in stars Anna May Wong and John Longden sharing a kiss. In the USA, however, the scenes were cut by the censor on the grounds that a kiss between a Chinese woman and an English man could be considered offensive. Much later, the interracial kiss in *Island in the Sun* (1957) saw the movie banned in Alabama as "Communist propaganda promoting race mongrelization". Credit for the first interracial kiss on US television goes to the 1968 *Star Trek* episode *Plato's Stepchildren*, when William Shatner (Captain Kirk) kissed Nichelle Nichols (Uhura).

One of the earliest seemingly lesbian kisses in the US cinema came in Josef von Sternberg's *Morocco* (1930), where Marlene Dietrich kisses another woman on the lips. The scene was reportedly Dietrich's own idea, and she was apparently also responsible for devising the ruse whereby the censors were blocked from cutting it: immediately before the kiss, she takes from the woman a flower, which she then gives to the indubitably masculine Gary Cooper; without the earlier segment, the producers were able to claim, the later one wouldn't make sense.

GREAT MOVIE POSTER TAGLINES

"No man has ever seen his like – No woman has ever felt his white-hot kiss!" – *Frankenstein* (1931)

"Dangerous to kiss!" – *Lady from Nowhere* (1936)

"She kisses and tells on the Class of 1940!" – *All Women Have Secrets* (1939)

"From blissful kisses to sizzling hisses, they're Mr and Mrs again!" – *Love Crazy* (1941)

"She'll kiss at the drop of a military secret – and SHE KNOWS ALL THE BEST FIRING SQUADS!" – *Careful, Soft Shoulders* (1942)

"He kissed her all over the map on another fellow's honeymoon!" – *Once Upon a Honeymoon* (1942)

"He's sweet 35 and never been kissed!" – *He Hired the Boss* (1943)

"You can't kiss away a murder!" – *Double Indemnity* (1944)

"You won't know whether to kiss 'em – or kill 'em!" – *Come Out Fighting* (1945)

"They say she kissed 2000 men!"
— *Down to Earth* (1947)

"The biggest kiss in movie history!"
— *That Midnight Kiss* (1949)

"Women fought for his kisses! Men clamored for
his life!" — *The Baron of Arizona* (1950)

"She became a woman in the middle of a kiss!"
— *The Member of the Wedding* (1952)

"She's learning to kiss — with a French accent!"
— *Pardon My French* (1952)

"Even when he kissed her he held a gun!"
— *A Good Day for a Hanging* (1959)

"They's more than kissin' cousins!"
— *All the Lovin' Kinfolk* (1970)

"Because Dandy couldn't stop with just a goodnight
kiss . . . this film must be rated X!" — *Dandy* (1972)

"They kiss and they tease, but always they please!"
— *Vampire Hookers* (1979)

"Why you shouldn't kiss your dog!" — *Fluffy* (1995)

"When you're a princess, sometimes you've got to
kiss a lot of frogs!" — *Slipper* (2001)

"The woman you never kiss is the woman you kiss
forever!" — *Murder on the Yellow Brick Road* (2005)

An unexpected difficulty occurred during the run of the 1974–75 US television series *Get Christie Love*, in which Teresa Graves starred in the title role as a sexy cop. Graves became a Jehovah's Witness and refused to do any more on-screen kissing with her male co-stars.

A running joke in the Oscar-winning stop-motion animated movie *Chicken Run* (2000) is that, every time the two chickens Rocky and Ginger are about to kiss, something interrupts them. This was because the moviemakers were concerned that to portray two chickens kissing on-screen might be simply to invite ridicule. When the characters eventually do achieve a kiss, their amorous beak-touching is carefully hidden from view.

For the notorious scene in Sidney Lumet's 1982 movie *Deathtrap* in which stars Michael Caine and Christopher Reeve kiss each other, both actors admitted later that they had to get roaring drunk before being uninhibited enough to go through with it.

The actress Capucine complained about her kissing scenes with Laurence Harvey in *Walk on the Wild Side* (1962), saying he "was not manly enough" for her. Harvey retorted: "Perhaps if you were more of a woman, I would be more of a man."

The 2004 movie *50 First Dates* was originally titled *50 First Kisses*.

"A woman has got to love a bad man once or twice
in her life to be thankful for a good one."
Mae West

——————— ST VALENTINE'S DAY ———————

On the Feast of St Valentine, February 14, the most romantic day of the year, lovers traditionally exchange gifts and cards. The custom, however, sprang up only during the 14th century, and seems to have little to do with any saint, more to do with the fact that February 14 was believed to be the day when birds began their mating season.

At least three St Valentines have been acknowledged by the Catholic Church. Two were said to have been martyred in Rome during the reign of Claudius II, the Goth, around the year 269. One of these was supposed to have been a priest of Rome, the other the Bishop of Turin. A third martyred St Valentine was said to have been a bishop in North Africa.

That at least one of the Valentines supposedly martyred in Rome may have had historical reality is attested to by a note of English chronicler William of Malmesbury (c1090–c1143) that in his time Rome's Flaminian Gate was called the Gate of St Valentine, named for a nearby church dedicated to the martyr and supposedly founded upon the site of his martyrdom.

Once the association between romance and St Valentine's Day had sprung up, various legends were invented about the supposed martyr. In one, he and St Marius were put to death for arranging secret Christian marriages forRoman soldiers at a time when such marriages had been banned by Claudius II. In another, he was condemned to death because active in clandestine efforts to free jailed Christians. Yet another was that he cured the daughter of one of his jailers of blindness, and that she fell in love with him. The night before his execution he sent her a note signed: "From your Valentine."

There is another Valentine – and one with a secure place in history – who might just have contributed to the connection between Valentine's Day and romance. This was a Gnostic called Valentinius, who was a candidate for Bishop of Rome in AD143. He taught that the act of marital lovemaking was one of the sacraments. This concept didn't enter the mainstream of early Christian teaching.

The link between February 14 and the choosing of lovers goes back much further. In Roman times, the fertility festival of Lupercalia began on February 15. February 15 itself was dedicated to the fertility god Lupercus; on that day his priests sacrificed goats to Romulus and Remus. Boys then ran through the city holding bloody strips of goatskin aloft. Women touched by the skins would, it was believed, have easy conception, pregnancy and childbirth. The eve of this feast, February 14, was a holiday dedicated to the goddess Juno Februata, an aspect of the Mother of the Gods whose province was passionate love. On February 14 youths drew lots to determine which young woman would be their amatory companion for the duration of the ensuing Lupercalia festivities. It was not uncommon for such temporary relationships to blossom into permanent ones. This pagan custom survived well into the Christian era. In 496 Pope Gelasius I declared February 14 to be St Valentine's Day, possibly to de-paganize the existing practice. The stunning failure of such de-paganizing attempts is evidenced by the fact that one of the most popular symbols on valentine cards even today is the Roman god Cupid, while the custom of men giving women red roses as a valentine gift has its origins in the red rose being favoured by Venus, the Roman goddess of love.

At least as late as the 18th century the method of choosing one's valentine was still by drawing lots. The practice of the man giving a gift to his valentine seems to date from about the 17th century, and appears to have eventually put an end to the lottery system, since many men balked at the notion of buying a possibly expensive gift for a woman who might turn out entirely incompatible.

The first known valentine was a poem written in 1415 by Charles, Duc d'Orléans (1391–1465), to his wife Isabella; the manuscript is now in the collection of the British Library (along with about 60 other poems he wrote for Isabella at this time). Charles had been imprisoned by the English in the Tower of London following the French defeat at the Battle of Agincourt.

The first printed valentine cards appeared in Britain late in the 18th century, and swiftly became very popular. These were a far cry from the modern mass-produced printed cards. Instead, they were often extremely elaborate manually assembled concoctions, complete with embossed papers, hand-coloured illustrations, laces, glass beads, bird feathers and much else. Even once mass-produced printed valentine cards had come into fashion, it was customary to use them merely as the basis for more ostentatious constructions.

A great surge in the popularity of the valentine card came in 1840 with the introduction in Britain of the Penny Post. Before then, mailing letters and other items was expensive, with the cost being paid by the recipient, and so the exchange of valentine cards was almost always restricted to those who could deliver by hand – stiffing an intended sweetheart with a postage-due bill was regarded as hardly favouring a successful suit.

The valentine card came to the USA from Britain during the 19th century. The first commercial valentine cards to be made in the New World were produced around 1847 by Esther A. Howland (1828–1904), the daughter of a stationer in Worcester, Massachusetts; before then her father had imported manufactured valentine cards from Britain. In her first year of trading, Howland sold $5000's worth of her elaborately made cards, and an industry was born. In 2001 the Greeting Card Association of America instituted an annual award named in her honour for a "Greeting Card Visionary".

It is estimated that the annual worldwide sales of valentine cards currently number about one billion, of which some 85% are bought by women. This means that more cards are sent in connection with St Valentine's Day than with any other festival of the year except Christmas (over 2.5 billion).

The USA was also the source of the offensive cards known as "vinegar valentines". These were originated by the New York printer John McLaughlin, and were noted for the cheapness of their production and most especially for the nastiness of the verses within; designed to be sent spitefully by suitors to women who spurned them, they were full of insults and warned of the miseries of spinsterhood.

At the other end of the scale were the hugely popular valentine cards using art by British illustrator Kate Greenaway (1846–1901). Her greetings-card illustrations came at a fairly early stage of her career, when she produced at least 32 sets of cards, each comprising 4–6 illustrations, for printer/publisher Marcus Ward. These cards were intended for various festivals, including Christmas and New Year, with Valentine's Day prominent among them.

In the early 20th century the photographic valentine became especially popular in Britain. In these a real photograph – often a photo of the sender – was hand-coloured by workers at the photographer's studio and pasted onto a printed postcard backing.

Introduced fairly recently to Japan and Korea, the custom of Valentine's Day has there taken a rather different turn, in that the gifts – usually chocolates – are exclusively given from women to men, and are often a matter of obligation rather than choice, as when working women are essentially compelled to give these gifts to all their male colleagues. A less than wholly successful attempt to counter the obvious unfairness of this has been the introduction of White Day, March 14, when men are supposed to give "something white" (often underwear) to all the women they know; in practice most men give these gifts only to their girlfriends or as an act of wooing.

In 1969 the Catholic Church removed St Valentine's Day from its calendar, among those of many other hitherto-recognized saints, on the grounds that the stories of St Valentine had no sound historical basis.

"Love is stronger than justice."
Dinah Shore

SEDUCTION

The word "flirt" comes from the Old French *conter fleurette*, which means to try to seduce by strewing flower petals.

The interplay between seduction and power is a curious one. Seduction is a power game more than a sexual one; at the same time, there are countless examples through history of people using their powers of seduction in order to gain or manipulate power.

Perhaps the most effective seducer of all time was the Egyptian queen Cleopatra (69–30BC). The wild tales of her sexual excesses are almost certainly slanderous myths; she was far too skilled a power-player to risk subverting her own efforts. But her use of seduction in the pursuit of power, first with Julius Caesar and then later, after Caesar's assassination in 44BC, with Mark Antony, is well documented.

A seducer whose name has entered the English language was the Italian adventurer Giacomo Girolamo Casanova de Seingalt (1725–1798). In his *Mémoires écrits par lui-même* – published posthumously in 1828-38 – he recounted numerous of his countless sexual seductions during a life that would have been quite adventurous enough even without them. In Casanova's case, the motivation for seduction seems to have been purely the exercise of personal power over women rather than enjoyment of the sexual act itself, and indeed some of his "seductions" would today be classified as rapes.

The "mad monk" Grigoriy Rasputin (c1871–1916) used a combination of psychological and sexual seduction, mixed in with a lot of mysticism and perhaps some hypnosis, in order to exercise a dominating influence over the court of Nicholas II and Alexandra. So overendowed with "presence" was Rasputin that legends of his supernatural abilities abounded; it has been recorded by otherwise sober scholars that his eventual assassins, on the eve of the Russian Revolution, had very considerable difficulty in getting him to actually stay dead. Of similar historical status is the information that he was hung like an extremely fortunate horse.

A latter-day Cleopatra, albeit on a much less exalted scale, was the Dutch-born French dancer Mata Hari (Margarete Gertrude Zelle; 1876–1917). She put her sexually seductive abilities to use in the cause of social climbing, taking numerous lovers among high political and military circles, and, particularly after the outbreak of World War I, turned these skills towards the service of espionage, which she conducted for both sides. In the end the French felt they'd put up with her long enough and shot her.

Creative artists have often used the aura of power granted them by their prestige to pursue Casanova-like careers of sexual seduction. Two of the more prominent examples have been the Belgian-born French novelist Georges Simenon (1903–1989) and the Spanish painter Pablo Picasso (1881–1973), both of whom claimed seductions in the thousands. Again as with Casanova, their motivation seems to have had more to do with the exercise of power and domination – and the tedious accumulation of numerical achievements – than with any particular pleasure in the sex act itself.

Another latter-day Casanova was the Irish adventurer, journalist and writer Frank Harris (1856–1931), who seems to have suffered from the condition now recognized as sexual addiction. Although his journalistic career was distinguished, it has been overshadowed by his career as a seducer, as recounted in his self-aggrandizing autobiography *My Life and Loves* (1923–27), which was for a long while banned as pornography.

The original of the legendary seducer Don Juan was supposedly one Don Juan Tenorio, a native of Seville, Spain, who lived during the 14th century. Numerous adaptations have been made of the legend, notably Gluck's ballet-pantomime *Don Juan* (1761), Mozart's opera *Don Giovanni* (1787), Tirso de Molina's play *El Burlador de Sevilla* (1634) and especially Lord Byron's unfinished epic poem *Don Juan* (1819–24). The latter is a peculiarly sympathetic portrayal, perhaps reflecting Byron's own reputation as a psychological as well as sexual seducer

LOVE POTIONS
AND APHRODISIACS

There is a distinction to be made. The aim of a love potion or philtre is to cause one person to fall in love with another, or two people to fall in love with each other; the physical consummation of that love, it is assumed, will take care of itself at the appropriate time(s). A love potion is therefore a very *personalized* device; it is also assumed to be magical in nature.

An aphrodisiac is concerned less with love than with lust, and it's *impersonal*. The individual aroused by an aphrodisiac will, it is assumed, be none too picky about the choice of partners; any personalization will come about through circumstances.

A further distinction should be made between aphrodisiacs and drugs used to counter erectile dysfunction. In the latter the assumption is that desire is there: only the ability needs assistance.

—— LOVE POTIONS IN LEGEND ——

The Greek hero Hercules was happily married to Deianira. She was abducted by the centaur Nexus, and Hercules gave chase, shooting Nexus with a poison-tipped arrow. As the centaur lay dying, he told Deianira to save some of his blood: this, he said, she could give to Hercules as a love potion if ever she thought his fancy was wandering.

Later Deianira did indeed entertain such suspicions, and so she washed one of Hercules's shirts in the blood. But Nexus had tricked her, and the poison from Hercules's own arrow almost killed the hero.

Also in Greek mythology, the sea god Glaucus fell for a nymph, Scylla, who would have nothing to do with him. He begged the witch Circe for a love potion to give Scylla. As he pleaded, Circe herself fell in love with him, but he spurned her. Furious with the nymph, Circe dosed with poison a pool where Scylla bathed, transforming Scylla into the horrific monster that assailed Odysseus and his crew.

According to St Jerome, the Roman poet/philosopher Lucretius (c99–55BC) was driven to insanity by a love potion his wife Lucilia administered to him, and wrote his great rationalist work *De Natura Rerum* only during his rare moments of lucidity.

The most famous love-potion legend of all concerns Tristan and Isolde (Iseult). The young Isolde was, for political reasons, betrothed to King Mark of Cornwall, and Tristan was, as Mark's faithful knight, sent to fetch her. Isolde's maid Brangaene, suspecting there might be difficulty persuading Isolde to fall for the elderly Mark, brought along on the voyage a love potion, intending to dose Isolde at a deftly chosen moment. By unfortunate misunderstanding, Tristan and Isolde drank the potion together.

On arrival in Cornwall, Isolde was wed to Mark. Anticipating there'd be hell to pay when he discovered she was no virgin, she made sure Mark got roaring drunk on his wedding night and persuaded the still-virginal Brangaene to take her place in the matrimonial bed. Sure enough, Mark was none the wiser.

The effects of the potion never died, and much of the rest of the legend of Tristan and Isolde is taken up with Mark's attempts to reclaim his wife from her true lover.

A rather more sophisticated love potion appears in the tale *Cligés* by Chrétien de Troyes. Cligés's kingdom is usurped by his uncle, Alis, who also forces Cligés's true love, Fénice, to be his bride. Fénice's maid, Thessala, prepares a potion whereby Alis will only ever be able to have sex with Fénice in his dreams, which dreams he will be unable to distinguish from real events. This stratagem works . . . for a while.

In one version of the legend of Sigurd and Brynhild, the trouble starts because Gudrun – sister of Gunnar, King of the Nibelungs – falls in love with Sigurd. But Sigurd is betrothed to Brynhild. Gudrun prevails upon her mother to create a love potion, on drinking which Sigurd ignores his promises to Brynhild and proposes marriage instead to Gudrun. Worse, he tricks Brynhild into being forced to marry Gunnar.

Later, after Sigurd has been killed by Högni to avenge Brynhild's suicide, Brynhild's brother, the King of the Huns, demands from Gunnar, and is given, Gudrun's hand in marriage, a union she agrees to only because herself given a love potion. In due course, however, this potion wears off and Gudrun dedicates herself to killing her spouse and avenging Sigurd's death.

The plot of the early Gilbert & Sullivan operetta *The Sorcerer* (1877) depends entirely on a love potion. Alexis and Aline are to marry. Alexis believes marriage should be a matter of love, not social station, and plots with Aline to administer, as a prank, a love potion to the entire village. The couple engage the sorcerer John Wellington Wells, and lace a large public teapot with potion. At first all goes to plan, but then complications ensue in the usual Gilbertian way; one is that Aline falls out of love with Alexis and into love with the local vicar . . .

APHRODISIACS

Many foods and drinks are popularly reputed to have aphrodisiac properties. It's worth noting, though, that physical exercise is known to increase the release of endorphins in the brain, thereby affecting the production of sex-related hormones. In women, research has shown, regular exercise leads to easier arousal and quicker orgasms. A suitable form of exercise is dancing . . . so the tradition of lovers going to the ball is not without a rational underpinning. ·

A survey carried out in the 1970s by a UK consumer magazine found that the most effective aphrodisiac of all was a bottle of wine shared between two.

By the way, folks, the author is not recommending you try (most of) these at home …

Acorns Use powdered in muscadel.

Alcohol Lowers inhibitions, so is effective in that context, but also decreases sensitivity, which can lead to loss of enjoyment and even, in men, ability.

Antlers Powdered and sprinkled on food or drink. The reputation is purely because of the shape.

Apricots According to the ancient Chinese.

Asparagus Rich in vitamin E, believed to aid production of the sex hormones. In 19th-century France it was obligatory for bridegrooms to devour large quantities before their wedding night.

Cannabis Efficacious in that it lowers inhibitions – much as does alcohol. Of course, it's illegal in some countries.

Cantharidin (Spanish Fly) Made from the dried, powdered body of the cantharides beetle, this irritates the urinary tract and thus increases blood flow to the penis; it is, however, a potentially lethal poison (illegal in many countries) and **should be avoided at all costs**.

Carbohydrates Eating carbohydrates increases energy levels and also the level of the brain's seratonin, which latter chemical has a mood-enhancing effect.

Cardamom Recommended in India, mixed with honey and milk, to counter impotence and premature ejaculation.

Celery Contains the male hormone androsterone, which acts as a pheromone when released in the sweat.

Chili peppers Contain capsaicin, which may trigger the

release of endorphins and thereby make you psychologically receptive to thoughts of lovemaking.

Chocolate Contains phenylethylamine, which can have similar effects to the body's own endorphins.

Cocaine Any aphrodisiac effects this might have are overwhelmingly outweighed by all the obvious disbenefits: **should be avoided at all costs.**

Cowcod soup A Jamaican brew including white rum, bananas and peppers.

Cucumbers As a food, the reputation is solely because of the shape. However, the smell of cucumbers has been shown to have an arousing effect on women.

Damiana (Wild Yam) Contains chemicals that may sensitize the genitals.

Deadly nightshade Another that **should be avoided at all costs.**

Donuts Not the consumption but the smell increases the flow of blood to the male genitals.

Figs Because of their shape: opened out, they resemble the vagina. Eating them can thus be a sensual experience, which may indeed have an aphrodisiac effect.

Fish A high-protein meal increases the level of tyrosine in the blood, which in turn increases epinephrine production in the brain. Fish also contain iodine and phosphorus in good quantity, which may enhance sexual performance.

Garlic Recommended in ancient cultures all over the world and quite possibly, through its general effectiveness as a medicinal plant and health-promoter, of genuine aphrodisiac utility.

Ginger Like garlic, a general promoter of health, and traditionally regarded as an aphrodisiac. The practice of making gingerbread men originated in the European belief that women who ate them would attract men.

Gingko Stimulates release of nitric acid, dilating the blood vessels and thereby improving blood flow, including to the genitals.

Honey A general health-promoter, packed with nutritional goodies, and perhaps aphrodisiac as a side-effect. The term "honeymoon" may derive from a European practice whereby couples would drink mead – honey wine – for a month after their wedding.

Irish moss (Carrageen) Taken as an infusion of the seaweed.

Jellyfish But only some varieties.

Lampreys Much favoured as an aphrodisiac by the Romans. King Henry I of England died in 1135 of eating a surfeit of them.

Licorice Not the consumption but the smell of black licorice increases the flow of blood to the male genitals.

Mandrake Presumably thought to be aphrodisiac because of its shape, which can resemble the human form; can be poisonous so **should be avoided at all costs.**

Mannish water A popular aphrodisiac in the Caribbean, a soup made from the head of a goat.

Meat A high-protein meal increases the level of tyrosine in the blood, which in turn increases epinephrine production in the brain.

Mistletoe Because the plant's berries emit a semen-like liquid when squeezed.

Nutmeg Recommended by several ancient cultures, especially mixed with egg and honey.

Onions Traditionally recommended for all the same reasons as garlic, which is of the same family.

Oysters A good source of zinc, which is involved in the body's production of testosterone, a hormone that increases both male and female libido. Zinc also helps increase sperm count.

Pepper Traditionally regarded as, dried and powdered, enhancing the effects of various other aphrodisiacs when used in combination with them. May have a genuine effect through stimulating blood flow.

Racahout Invented in the late 19th century by US gynaecologist George Napheys, and made by mixing cacao and starch, with vanilla as flavouring.

Rhinoceros horn Powdered; assumed to be aphrodisiac because of the shape. There's no scientific basis, and the various types of rhinoceros are endangered.

Roses The second most popular cut flower in the USA after lilies, with a high proportion being given as love gifts – sales receipts soar around Valentine's Day. The edible petals in particular have a long history of use in love philtres.

Royal jelly The stuff worker bees feed to the queen, supposedly the reason she lives fifty times longer than other bees. Packed with nutrients, it is thought to be beneficial to the human reproductive system in general, but its effects are far more widespread. It contains: acetylcholine, aspartic acid, ecanoic acid and gamma globulin; vitamins A, C, D and E, plus many of the B complex; essential amino acids the human body does not produce; calcium and iron; nucleic acids.

Saffron A traditional recommendation in many cultures. May stimulate sensitivity.

Snails Recommended by the ancient Greeks.

Testicles Either animal or human.

Tiger Various parts of the tiger are reputed in the Far East to have aphrodisiac properties. There is no scientific basis for such belief, and tigers are endangered.

Tongkat ali A tree found in Malaysia, Burma, Thailand and Indonesia whose taproot is reputed to have aphrodisiac qualities rather like ginseng's.

Truffles Pigs root for truffles because the smell has chemicals akin to that of the male porcine sex hormones. For this reason it's thought truffles may enhance sexual performance in human males, too.

Unagi Raw sea eel, a sushi delicacy reputed in Japan to be an aphrodisiac.

Vanilla The name comes via Spanish (*vainilla*, diminutive of *vaina*) from the Latin word *vagina*, meaning a sheath.

Water Drinking several glasses a day of plain water is beneficial to the whole cardiovascular system, and thereby may have some aphrodisiac effect.

Yohimbé bark Drunk as a tea, this increases testosterone levels, stimulates the nervous system and increases blood flow to the penis; it should, however, be used with care, especially by those suffering heart disease and hypertension.

Zucchini (courgettes) Long regarded as an aphrodisiac because of the shape.

ANTI-APHRODISIACS

Urban legends are full of substances reputed to dampen desire, such as the mysterious "bromide" inflicted on school-boys and soldiers alike. The 19th-century US sexologist Orson Scott Fowler advised that a forty-day regime of a drink made from white waterlilies would banish erections for life.

Here are two scientifically proven longer-term anti-aphrodisiacs:

Cholesterol High cholesterol levels, because clogging of the arteries leads to sluggish blood flow, are a primary cause of erectile dysfunction.

Tobacco smoking As with cholesterol, this inhibits the flow of blood, including to the genital regions.

"Love is the irresistible desire to be irresistibly desired."
Robert Frost

FURTHER APHRODISIAC OPTIONS

If you've tried all the previous without success,
here are some further traditional recommendations
you might consider.

Almonds, anchovies, anise, ants, artichokes
– bamboo shoots, bananas, banisterine, barley,
basil, beans, beef, Benedictine, birds-nest soup, bitters,
blood (preferably human), bone marrow, brains
(especially human), butter – cabbage, caperberry,
capsicum, caraway , carp, carrots, caviar, chameleons,
Chartreuse, cheese, chestnuts, chives, cinnamon,
clams, cloves, cockles, cod röe, coffee, conch,
coriander, courgettes, crabs, crayfish, cress, crysmon,
cubeb, cuckoo-pint – darrel, dates, dill,
doves' brains – eels, eggs, elecampine, eringoes –
fennel – gherkins, gillyflower, ginseng, goat milk,
goose tongues – jimsonweed, juniper – kumquats –
leeks, lentils, liver, lobsters, lycopodium – marjoram,
mescaline, milk, mint, mushrooms, mussels,
mustard, mutton, myristica – nuts – pansies, parsley,
parsnips, *pâté de fois gras*, peas, periwinkles,
pine nuts, pistachio nuts, plovers' eggs,
pomegranates, potatoes, prawns, prunes –
quebracho, quince – radishes, red mullet, rice, rye
bread – sabal, salmon, satyrion, saw palmetto,
scallions, scallops, scuraum, shallots, shrimp, skink,
snakes, spinach – tarragon, thornapple, thyme,
tobacco, tomatoes, trout, turmeric, turnera,
turnips – valerian, veal, venison, verbena – walnuts,
wheat, wine – yarrow.

—————— LOVE AND THE STARS ——————

Most astrologers will tell you they cannot predict certain outcomes, only *likely* ones – that the future is as yet unwritten, so all they can really say is what current indicators suggest. This all sounds a little like romance itself, where the uncertainty of how exactly things will turn out is part of the delicious excitement yet only a fool would ignore any symptoms that all might end in tears.

Of course, astrology is not a science, whatever its adherents might claim: it has no testable theories, no plausible models of how any of its credos might actually work. Yet the notion that the time of year at which one is born might have an effect on later character traits is not ludicrous, and countless individuals have found love and romance through following the suggestions of astrology.

Each of the 12 signs of the Zodiac connects to one of the four traditional elements Earth, Air, Fire and Water:

Aries	Fire	March 21–April 19
Taurus	Earth	April 20–May 20
Gemini	Air	May 21–June 21
Cancer	Water	June 22–July 22
Leo	Fire	July 23–August 22
Virgo	Earth	August 23–September 22
Libra	Air	September 23–October 23
Scorpio	Water	October 24–November 21
Sagittarius	Fire	November 22–December 21
Capricorn	Earth	December 22–January 19
Aquarius	Air	January 20–February 18
Pisces	Water	February 19–March 20

Because of the revolution of the Earth around the Sun each year, the Sun appears to follow a slow path through the heavens, passing through each of the 12 constellations of the Zodiac in turn. Your Sun sign is the constellation in which the Sun appeared to be at the time of your birth.

Each of the four elements is said to be complementary to one of the others. The four elements thus form two pairs:

Fire with Air
Earth with Water

Signs of the same element are said to be *trine* to each other, while signs of complementary elements are said to be *sextile* to each other. Thus:

Aries, Leo and Sagittarius are trine
Taurus, Virgo and Capricorn are trine
Gemini, Libra and Aquarius are trine
Cancer, Scorpio and Pisces are trine

With the sextile signs it is not so easy to draw up a simple little table, because a further factor comes into play. Signs exactly opposite each other in the Zodiac are said to be *in opposition* to each other, and this is more important than the sextile relationship. Thus:

Aries, Aquarius and Gemini are sextile
Taurus, Cancer and Pisces are sextile
Gemini, Aries and Leo are sextile
Cancer, Virgo and Taurus are sextile

while

Aries and Libra are in opposition
Taurus and Scorpio are in opposition
Gemini and Sagittarius are in opposition
Cancer and Capricorn are in opposition
Leo and Aquarius are in opposition
Virgo and Pisces are in opposition

"To get the full value of joy
You must have someone to divide it with."
Mark Twain

Couples whose Sun signs are in trine will generally get along very harmoniously with each other, as to a lesser extent will those whose signs are in sextile. If you and your partner have signs with either of these two relationships, you should be very comfortable with each other. However, "comfortable" is not necessarily the best quality for a lifelong love affair; depending upon your individual personality, you may be better off with a partner whose sign belongs to or is in opposition to an element that is *not* complementary to your own.

Further, Sun signs say little or nothing about attraction. (In this context we're talking about the attraction between personalities, not straightforward physical attraction, which is outwith the scope of astrology.) We all know plenty of people whose personalities are such that we get along very comfortably with them, but this doesn't mean we're likely to – or want to – fall in love with them!

To judge the likelihood of romantic attraction between couples, astrologers look also at other signs defined by the moment of each individual's birth. These characteristics include the positions of the planets in the Zodiac at the time of birth: a person born in early April will have a Sun sign of Aries, but their personality could also be affected by the planet Mars being in (for example) Gemini, the planet Venus being in (for example) Scorpio, and so on.

Generally far more important than the positions of the planets are (1) the position of the Moon and (2) the zodiacal constellation that was appearing over the horizon (because of the rotation of the Earth) at the moment of the individual's birth. This latter datum is called the *ascendant* sign.

Determining your Moon sign and your ascendant sign (not to mention your various planetary signs) requires knowledge of the exact time and location of your birth, followed by a great deal of complicated mathematics. Astrologers use standard diagrams to help work out the details of all this; these are the birth charts often mentioned in astrological lore.

So far as the ascendant is concerned, the general rule is that people will be attracted to each other very strongly – this is where the fireworks happen – when the Sun sign of one is the same as the ascendant sign of the other.

A more profound attraction is involved when it comes to considering the partners' Moon signs: fireworks are all very well in the short term, but the ideal is to find one's soulmate. Put simply, the Sun sign represents creative energy and the Moon sign represents emotional needs. Thus if one partner's Sun sign is the same as the other partner's Moon sign, then – all other things being favourable – a superb complementarity should exist between the two partners, with the one whose Sun sign is the same as the other's Moon sign being the more dominant.

Of course, it is perfectly possible – albeit rare – that each could have a Sun sign the same as the other's Moon sign. In that event, the profoundest love of all is possible.

The very simplified guidelines here are drawn from the occidental tradition of astrology. Other astrological systems exist, notably the Indian and Chinese systems.

---

*"Seduce my mind and you can have my body,
Find my soul and I'm yours forever."*
Anonymous

*"I don't want to live. I want to love first,
and live incidentally."*
Zelda Fitzgerald

ENGAGEMENT, MARRIAGE AND STAYING IN LOVE

MARRIAGE CUSTOMS

While the core of the Christian marriage service is of course prescribed by the Church – with secular versions in the West being based to a great extent upon their religious equivalents – many of the traditions associated with marriage have little or nothing to do with Christianity, and some date from long before it.

The word "bride" shares its root with the word "brew" or "brewer", Old German *bru* (English brew) and *brut* or *braut* (bride)..

The custom of exchanging rings to signify engagement may date back to a prehistoric practice still preserved in some traditional cultures today. During the marriage ceremony, the couple are tied together with grasses at the wrist and ankle to symbolize that they're "tied" together for life..

In ancient Egypt, before the appearance of specially minted coins, metal rings were used as money. When a man put a ring on the finger of his betrothed, he was stating that he trusted her to share his material possessions.

The wedding ring dates from later than the engagement ring, because in general the period between betrothal and marriage was brief so a single ring in effect served both purposes. However, in 1215 Pope Innocent III decreed that the interval should be extended, and so it became the practice for the bride to be given a second ring during the marriage ceremony to seal the contract initiated by the first.

The third finger has long been the traditional recipient of the betrothal and wedding rings. This dates back to the ancient Greek belief that love was routed to the heart via the principal vein in this finger. The custom was for a long time that the engagement ring was put on the third finger of the right hand, rather than the left, being moved to the left hand at the time of the marriage. In 1549 Edward VI of England decreed that the proper hand for the ring was the left, and thus it has remained since. In some European countries the engagement ring is worn on the left hand and transferred to the right hand on marriage.

In the times when marriage was regarded as a business transaction, with the groom purchasing the bride from her family, the betrothal ring was part of the purchase price and also, since it represented a sometimes substantial financial investment by the groom, a non-returnable down payment that affirmed his serious intent. It was also from this time that the practice began of the bride's father accompanying his daughter up the aisle to "give" her to the groom. The wedding symbolized the fulfilment of the contract, and the final act was the promised delivery of the bride.

The incorporation of diamonds into the betrothal ring began in Italy in the Middle Ages, although supposedly initiated in 1477 by Prince Maximilian of Austria (later Maximilian I,

Emperor of Germany) when he became betrothed to Mary of Burgundy (heiress of Charles the Bold); since this was an arranged political marriage *par excellence* – Mary brought him Burgundy and Flanders to add to his realm – the romantic associations are ironic.

The fancy was that diamonds could be fashioned only by the flames of love; further, the gem was associated with Venus, the goddess of love. In more practical terms, the incorporation of a diamond increased the financial value of the ring and thereby the insurance that the groom would not renege on the arrangement.

The exchange of wedding rings is not a requirement in civil marriages, but is in Christian ceremonies, having been prescribed by the Council of Trent in the 16th century.

When marriage was regarded as a business transaction, the counterpart of the bridal price paid by the groom or the groom's family was the dowry bequeathed to the couple by the bride's family. This could be financial in nature, and among wealthy and aristocratic families generally was, but for the rest it usually consisted of household goods and the like. Often the young woman herself would supplement the contributions of her parents by making or collecting further clothes and homemaking items.

The tradition of storing the dowry items in a special item of furniture called a "hope chest" is of indeterminate origin, and may be an American invention; the term is now often used to refer to the accumulation of goods itself, with no implications as to its storage. The French equivalent, *trousseau*, comes from the noun *trousse*, meaning "bundle".

The widespread practice of bundling is of ancient standing and is connected with the original idea of betrothal. Although today Western society, in a profound state of denial, assumes marriage signifies the onset of sexual relations, originally marriage signified rather that the couple intended to form the nucleus of a new family; it was regarded as if anything undesirable that the couple should not have engaged in lovemaking beforehand. Betrothal thus tokened the start of a longer-term sexual relationship between a couple, which would probably but not necessarily result in marriage and offspring; usually marriage waited until the woman became pregnant.

In bundling, when a young man and woman had passed through the stages of mere kissing, cuddling and petting, they graduated to sleeping together but with the man fully clothed and on top of rather than under the covers, where the woman slept. After perhaps some weeks, the young man was permitted to sleep at nights under the covers with the woman, but still fully clothed. The end of the progression was, of course, that the man and woman were both under the covers without the hindrance of clothes, and at this stage their betrothal was officially recognized.

The practice of bundling is often regarded as Scandinavian in origin, but this may simply be because it survived longer in that region than elsewhere; it has certainly been observed in most if not all European countries and far beyond. It was censured by the Christian Church, whose cultural influence spread with reasonable rapidity throughout the Mediterranean region but had greater difficulty penetrating the northern lands.

An important purpose of betrothal was to allow a premarital interval during which the families of bride and groom could hammer out details of the commercial contract for the transfer of ownership of the woman from father to husband. Initially the negotiations concerned the bride price that would be paid for the woman; in later centuries they were more often related to the nature of the dowry her father would pay.

The engagement party, or flouncing, was originally less of a party, more a preliminary council between the two families to start the discussion of the financial arrangements.

The practice of the man making a formal proposal of marriage to his intended, rather than to her family, is very recent in origin, its widespread adoption dating from the 19th century; before that, a declaration of love was interpreted as a desire to marry. The formal proposal to the bride's father is a hangover from the days of arranged marriages.

For a long while, it was common that the man would send friends to propose on his behalf rather than do so himself. *En route*, the friends would observe what or whom they encountered, interpreting such meetings as omens concerning the future happiness of the couple; they might even turn back if the omens appeared sufficiently bleak. Pigeons, nanny goats and wolves were regarded as favourable signs; pregnant women, blind people and monks were bad news.

The tradition of women rather than men being the ones to propose on February 29 dates from when, in English law, the leap year day had no legal recognition. The reasoning ran that, since other laws refused to recognize the day, so too should the "law" that it be men who took the initiative in matters of the heart.

In one Brittany proposal custom, the man could leave a branch of hawthorn on his intended's threshold on Mayday. To accept the proposal she would leave the branch in place; to reject the suitor, she substituted a cauliflower.

For a long while there was a belief that being betrothed more than once brought eternal damnation. This quasi-superstition was almost certainly invented by the Christian Church at a time when betrothal rather than marriage signified the onset of sexual relations.

The practice of publishing banns – public announcements of a forthcoming marriage – was instituted in an attempt to ensure there were no legal obstacles to the union. For the same reason weddings were (and are) public ceremonies, so that anyone who knew of a good reason why bride and groom should not be joined had a last chance to state it.

The stag party appears to be a custom as old as marriage itself, and to have originated independently in cultures all over the world. The Western practice may date back to ancient Sparta, where a soldier would hold a party on his wedding eve to indicate that his new allegiance to his spouse would not nullify his allegiance to his comrades-in-arms.

The practice of the bridal shower originated in Holland at an unknown date. If the bride's father disapproved of the intended union and thus withheld the dowry, friends and neighbours of the couple would gather together to shower the bride with appropriate gifts. The modern form of the bridal shower appears to have originated around the end of the 19th century.

Although the tradition of having a white bridal dress is supposedly to symbolize the bride's virgin purity, this is a recent conceit; it was popularized by Anne of Brittany when she married in white in 1499, and again by Queen Victoria when she wore a white dress at her wedding in 1840 (before then British royal brides had customarily worn silver dresses). From at least the time of the Saxons through until the 18th century a white dress symbolized poverty, being worn only by poor brides: the plainness and whiteness of the garment indicated she was bringing nothing to the marriage but herself.

Otherwise wedding dresses could be any colour, with red being popular in medieval Europe. Most often, the bride simply wore her best dress. However, colour symbolism crept in; for example, green signified youth and blue signified constancy, although green could also be considered both unlucky and an indicator of the bride's moral laxity (the colour symbolizing grass stains). Wedding attire never contained yellow, for that colour symbolized jealousy.

White dresses are never worn at weddings in the Far East, where white symbolizes mourning and death.

The customary holding of weddings and wedding celebrations on Saturday rather than Sunday – the previously favoured day – dates from the 17th century, when the Puritans condemned anything resembling fun being had on the Sabbath.

The bridal veil supposedly signifies youth, modesty and virginity, but again this is a relatively recent symbolism – although the custom of the bridal veil itself is an ancient one.

Among the ancient Greeks, Romans and Hebrews the veils were generally brightly coloured, and could be threaded with gold and silver. Among the Anglo-Saxons it was customary for the bride to wear her hair loose so that it acted as a veil. The early Christians took matters to extremes, draping both bride and groom in a canopy of cloth.

The popular Wedding March known colloquially as "Here Comes the Bride" is taken from the Bridal Chorus in the opera *Lohengrin* (1848), by Richard Wagner.

The role of best man dates from when men might abduct women to be their brides; they would take along their best and strongest friends to help defend against attempts by the young woman's family to recover her. The best man traditionally stands to the right of the bride and groom so as to leave his sword hand free in order to defend the marrying pair. For the same reason, the groom stands always to the right of the bride.

Bridesmaids were introduced to the bridal party in Roman times as a measure to trick evil spirits, who might otherwise seize and possess the bride. Confronted by a profusion of young women all dressed much alike, however, the spirits – who must have been astonishingly stupid as well as evil – grew sufficiently confused that they gave up their malevolent intents and wandered off to pester someone else.

The ringing of bells immediately at the conclusion of the wedding ceremony was supposed to drive away evil spirits that might otherwise threaten the marriage.

The custom of throwing confetti over newly wedded couples dates back to pre-Christian times, when it was the practice to cast grain and nuts at them to promote fecundity; the practice still persists in the frequent use of rice rather than paper confetti. In some cultures the approved "fertility missile" is eggs. From the same source sprang the custom of tossing sweetmeats over the happy couple – the Italian word *confetti* has the same root as the word for confectionery.

The throwing or giving of a shoe refers back as far as the ancient Assyrians and Hebrews, who would exchange shoes as an earnest of their integrity in a commercial bargain. A further symbolism of the shoe among the Anglo-Saxons was that it signified authority; the passing or throwing of a shoe from one person to another indicated a transfer of authority.

The good-luck attribute of wedding horseshoes is thought possibly to derive from their crescent shape, which refers to the crescent of the Moon – which has traditional connotations of fertility. The silver helps keep away witches and evil spirits, too. An inverted horseshoe brings bad rather than good luck: if the shoe is thought of as a vessel, it holds the good luck when its two tines are pointing upward, but lets it spill out when the "vessel" is tipped over.

The custom of the wedding cake is prehistoric in origin, and can be found in almost all cultures; the sharing of specially baked food has obvious connotations of fertility and good fortune. The single, large wedding cake is a fairly recent invention; before then the tradition was to pass around small cakes or biscuits, which could be eaten on the spot or taken home – or both – by the wedding guests. Single women would sleep with a piece of the wedding cake under their pillows in the belief that so doing would bring them a good husband.

From the taking home of these wedding sweetmeats sprang the custom of giving guests a piece of the cake to take home with them – and of sending cake to invitees unable to attend – and also the custom of giving the guests wedding favours. The most popular favours today are sugar-coated almonds, five in number, symbolizing health, fertility, wealth, happiness and longevity.

The precursor of the tiered wedding cake was invented by a French baker in late-17th-century England. Previously there

The practice of the bride tossing
her bouquet represents a
cleaning up of earlier customs.
The original practice, known as
flinging the stocking, is of
ancient origin: the wedding
guests would charge into the
room where the couple were
attempting to consummate their
union, grab the stockings of bride, groom, bridesmaids
and anyone else, and throw these over the entwined
couple.

Flinging the stocking was prettified in 14th-century
France into the custom of the bride, before departing
into married life with the groom, removing her garter
and tossing it to the men of the bridal party.
Unfortunately, this too could lead to disreputable
scenes, because the young and usually inebriated male
guests often tried to get hold of the garter before the
bride had actually removed it.

When the bouquet was substituted, the practice
became to throw it to the women of the party rather
than the men. The introduction of this custom served
two purposes, because before then it had been
common for female wedding guests to try to tear
pieces off the wedding dress as good-luck tokens.

For good luck in the marriage, the bride should toss
the bouquet back over her shoulder.

had been a practice whereby guests (rather than the hosts) brought small cakes to the wedding feast, stacking these on top of each other as a gift to the newlyweds. The baker merely shortcircuited this process by creating a single cake in the shape of the stack.

This evolved to become the three-tiered wedding cake, whose shape was designed in emulation of the spire on St Bride's Church near Ludgate Circus in London.

The tradition of the newlyweds feeding each other pieces of the wedding cake is older than that of the single, large wedding cake. The symbolism is that the couple will nourish each other for the rest of their lives. The joint first cutting of the cake symbolizes the jointness of their future endeavours together.

The garter of the bride was traditionally blue. This custom appears to have originated in England, where members of the Order of the Garter included a blue garter among their other ceremonial paraphernalia. The only women allowed as members of the Order were queens and princesses; however, every bride is queen on her wedding day.

Another antisocial custom practised by the wedding party upon the newlyweds is *shivare*, which was born in the Middle Ages and is still occasionally perpetrated today. While the couple are trying to concentrate on their first night together as man and wife, friends and family congregate outside the house to bang pots and pans, sound hooters, etc., and generally do their utmost to disrupt the proceedings within.

The carrying of the bride by the groom over the threshold appears to have arisen from the notion that evil spirits could lurk under thresholds; the groom was protecting his new wife from these. Also, it was believed to be an ill omen should a bride trip or stumble as she entered the home for the first time; carrying her obviated such mishaps.

The rhyme

Something old,
Something new,
Something borrowed,
Something blue,
And a silver sixpence
In your shoe

appears to have been penned in Victorian England, although little more is known about it. The traditions to which it refers are far older: the good-luck wedding gifts every couple should have.

The "something old" was traditionally a garter given to the bride by a married woman friend so that the happiness of one marriage would spread to the other. It also symbolizes the couple's existing friends, who should not become estranged because of the marriage.

The "something new" – the wedding presents – symbolizes prosperity in the couple's future.

The "something borrowed" is traditionally a valued heirloom belonging to the bride's family. Good luck is assured if she returns it.

And the "something blue" refers to an ancient Hebrew tradition whereby brides wore blue ribbons as symbols of their future fidelity.

The sixpenny piece, or sixpence, was a British coin that disappeared from circulation soon after the currency was decimalized in 1971. The placing of a sixpence in the bride's slipper was thought to ensure the marriage would be wealthy.

The origins of the word "honeymoon" are somewhat obscure. The most popular theory concerns the ancient custom in parts of Europe whereby a newly wed couple would drink *metheglin*, a kind of mead or honey wine, during the lunar month after the marriage. After his marriage to the Burgundian Princess Ildeco, Attila the Hun (c406–453) supposedly indulged in this custom so enthusiastically that he died of it.

Alternatively, "honeymoon" is a corruption of a Norse word meaning "hiding month". It was a relatively common practice for a man to abduct the bride of his choice from a neighbouring village and hide away with her until her family had calmed down enough for a bridal price to be discussed and the marriage formalized, or until she was demonstrably pregnant, at which point her family could be expected to make the best of a bad job.

A third theory, supported by the *Oxford English Dictionary* (which has been known to err), more prosaically points to the fact that the word isn't known to have entered the English language until the 16th century, when it seems to have derived from the notion that the period immediately after marriage was all sweetness and honey, but in due course love would, like the full Moon, wane.

"To love is so startling it leaves little time for anything else."
Emily Dickinson

"Love and work are the cornerstones of our humanness."
Sigmund Freud

THE PATRON SAINTS OF
LOVE AND MARRIAGE

Of the two saints whose responsibilities include lovers, by far the better known is St Valentine, supposedly martyred by beheading in Rome around the year 269 and buried on the Flaminian Way, though later his remains were removed to the Church of St Praxedes. There's some confusion about his life, to the extent that he's usually regarded as two different saints: St Valentine of Terni and St Valentine of Rome.

The second patron saint of lovers is St Dwynwen (her name is also rendered as Donwen, Donwenna, Dunwen and Dwyn), who died around the year 460. The daughter of the Welsh King Brychan, she was renowned for her beauty and piety. Though she was determined to be a nun, she and a young man fell in love with each other. In a dream, she was given a drink that released her from love's spell, but it also turned the young man to ice. She therefore prayed that his heart be rekindled elsewhere, and that all lovers should find true happiness.

A well called Ffynnon Dwynwen was dedicated to her. Lovers came from far and wide to make their wishes here and to ask the eels of the well what the future held.

St Valentine is also the patron saint of happy marriages, in that happily married couples are, of course, lovers. The patron saint of married couples *per se* is St Joseph, the husband of the Virgin Mary.

There are many patron saints of brides. What may be a partial list is: St Adelaide, St Blaesilla, St Catherine of Genoa, St Clotilde, St Delphina, St Dorothy of Caesarea, St Dorothy of Montau, St Elizabeth of Hungary, St Elizabeth of Portugal,

St Hedwig, St Ida of Herzfeld, St Ivetta of Huy, St Margaret the Barefooted and (a rare male) St Nicholas of Myra.

The patron saint of married women is St Monica, who was born in 322 in Algeria and died in 387 at Ostia, in Italy. She was the mother of St Augustine of Hippo. Although born a Christian, she was given in marriage to a pagan, Patricius, who seems to have been a brute; nevertheless, she succeeded in converting him on his deathbed. Her other significant conversion was, of course, that of her son Augustine, who until then had led a dissolute life. As a reformed alcoholic, St Monica obviously has other patronly responsibilities.

There are two patron saints of second marriage, St Adelaide and St Matilda. They were related by marriage: St Matilda, who was born in 895 and died in 968, was the mother-in-law of St Adelaide, who was born about 931 and died in 999.

St Matilda's father was Count Dietrich of Westphalia and her mother Reinhild of Denmark. In 913 she married the Saxon King Henry the Fowler in 913, whose prior marriage had been annulled. She bore him an illustrious brood of children: the Holy Roman Emperor Otto the Great, St Bruno, Gerberga, who was Louis IV's queen, and Hedwig, who married Hugh the Great and by him bore Hugh Capet, elected King of France in 987. Matilda was renowned for comforting the sick, visiting prisoners, and teaching the poor.

St Adelaide was daughter of the Burgundian King Rupert II. Her first marriage was to Lothair, who in due course succeeded to the throne of Italy. After Lothair's death, she wed the Holy Roman Emperor Otto the Great. When he in turn died, she became, after some squabbling, Empress in his stead, and spent much of the rest of her life doing good deeds for the poor and evangelizing in the name of Christianity. She spent her final years as a nun.

There are far more patron saints of difficult marriages than there are of happy ones, the need being greater. Here is what may be a partial listing: St Castora Gabrielli , St Catherine of Genoa, St Dorothy of Montau, St Edward the Confessor, St Elizabeth of Portugal, St Fabiola, St Gengulphus, St Godelieve, St Gummarus, St Hedwig, St Helena, St Louis IX, St Margaret the Barefooted, St Marguerite d'Youville, St Monica, St Nicholas of Flue, St Olaf II, St Pharaildis, St Philip Howard, St Radegunde, St Rita of Cascia, St Theodore of Sykeon, St Thomas More, St Wilgefortis and St Zedislava Berka.

PATRON SAINTS FOR THE RESISTING
— OF —
SEXUAL TEMPTATION

And there are plenty of these, too, again for obvious reasons. Most important is St Mary Magdalene, also known as the Sinner – although much modern research suggests that she was, rather, Christ's most trusted disciple. She is also a patron saint of reformed prostitutes.

The Italian St Angela of Foligno (1248–1309) was born a pagan, but in 1285 was converted to Christianity by a vision. Before then she had married young and carried on a wild and adulterous existence. Post-conversion, she was a reformed character, devoting herself to God and becoming famous for her mystical writings, her humility and her charity.

Also Italian, St Catherine of Siena (1347–1380) was another visionary, and one who rose high within the Church, being a counsellor to two popes: Gregory XI and Urban VI. She devoted herself to God after experiencing a vision at the age of six, but her best-known vision came in later life, when she saw herself being given a wedding ring by Christ. This mystical form of marriage is echoed today in the expression, regarding nuns, that they are married to Christ.

St Margaret of Cortona (1247–1297) was yet another Italian. She fled from home in her teens to be mistress of a young aristocrat. In 1274 her lover was murdered, and Margaret believed this was a message from God telling her she had sinned. She and her young son took refuge in a friary, where she had to struggle to resist the many attempted seductions that came her way.

Margaret devoted herself to the poor and sick, and in 1286, some while after herself entering the Church, was given a charter to work with them, founding the order known as the Poor Ones and a hospital in Cortona.

She is also a patron saint of reformed prostitutes.

St Mary of Edessa was a niece of the Mesopotamian St Abraham Kidunaia (c296–c366), who spent most of his life living in solitude in a cell. Mary lived nearby, also in piety, for the first twenty years of her life, but was then seduced by a passing renegade monk. In shame she fled to a distant city, where she gave herself over to a life of promiscuity and probably prostitution. St Abraham travelled to the city in the guise of a soldier and allowed himself to be picked up by her. In her home, he persuaded her to give up her sinful ways, and she spent the rest of her life in penitence.

St Mary of Egypt (c344–c421), born to a rich family, ran away from home at the age of twelve and became a singer and prostitute in Alexandria. After 17 years of this she accompanied a pilgrimage to Palestine, gaining clients among the pilgrims. On the Feast of the Exaltation of the Cross, she found herself unable to enter a church; repenting her sins, she called upon the Virgin Mary, who told her she must cross the Jordan to find salvation. This Mary did, spending the rest of her life in the desert as a hermit.

She is also a patron saint of reformed prostitutes.

St Pelagia of Antioch was a young woman and a disciple of St Lucian of Antioch when, around 311, soldiers arrived to arrest her. Believing she was going to be raped, she persuaded them to let her go upstairs to change her clothing, then threw herself out of a high window.

PATRON SAINTS FOR FERTILITY

To help with difficulties in conceiving, women can call on one or all of these: St Agatha, St Anne, St Anthony of Padua, St Casilda of Toledo, St Felicity, St Fiacre, St Francis of Paola, St Giles, St Henry II, St Margaret of Antioch, St Medard, St Philomena, St Rita of Cascia, St Theobald of Alba.

"One word frees us
Of all the weight and pain in life,
That word is Love "
Socrates

"We can do no great things
– only small things with great love."
Mother Teresa of Calcutta

"Love is like linen often changed, the sweeter."
Phineas Fletcher

DEITIES OF LOVE, ROMANCE, FERTILITY AND SEX

If all else fails in matters of the heart, you might do worse than to call upon some of these for assistance.

Aine Irish goddess of love and of fertility. Came to be regarded as a fairy queen.

Aizen–Myo'o Japanese god of love, shown with a lion's head in his hair and a third, vertical eye between his two normal ones.

Ala Among the Ibo of Nigeria, the Earth goddess, thus goddess of both fertility and death.

Alpan Etruscan goddess of sexual love, also of the underworld. Usually shown wearing jewellery but otherwise nude, or nude under a loose cloak and sandals.

Amma Dogon fertility god, also the god of rain. Creator of the universe as an egg, from which came a twinned male and female. Later he raped the Earth; anguished when his penis encountered an ants' nest, he plucked out the nest, thereby giving rise to the practice of female circumcision. The son of the rape, Yuruga, committed incest with the Earth, thereby giving rise to menstruation. Disgusted, Amma created four men and four women to populate the world, and departed.

Amun Egyptian god of sex and fertility. He began as the local Theban god Nut Amun, being progressively more associated with fertility and sexuality as he rose to prominence. He became the patron god of the Pharaohs, and was combined with the sun god Ra to form Amun-Ra, the ruler of all the gods. Much later, Alexander the Great, after consulting the oracle of Amun, added "Son of Amun" to his own titles.

Ana (or **Anu**) Irish mother of the gods and a fertility goddess. Two twin hills near Killarney are called the Paps of Anu.

Anahita (or **Anaitis**, **Aredvi Sura**) Persian fertility goddess, also a goddess of war and water. Paradoxically, usually shown as a virgin.

Anat (or **Anata**, **Anath**) Goddess of sexuality, fertility, war and hunting in various cultures, notably Syrian, Phoenician and Egyptian. She was sister or niece (accounts vary) of Baal, and later became identified with Astarte (otherwise identified as her sister) and Asherah. Usually depicted naked, often bearing weaponry.

Angus (or **Aengus**, **Anghus**, **Angus Og**, **Oengus Mac Oc**) Irish god of love. Four songbirds ever flew around his head; all who heard them fell in love. In a dream he saw a maiden with whom he fell in love. Waking, he had his mother and father search Ireland for her, and at length she was found by a servant of his father's. He was shown 150 maidens and immediately identified her; her name was Caer. The maidens were turned into swans for a year, and Angus was told, if he could identify Caer as a swan, he could marry her. Finding her, he transformed himself into a swan so they could be together.

Anteros Greek god created as a companion to Eros, who was lonely because love cannot exist in isolation. (The name Anteros means "returned love".) Anteros is the enemy of those who do not respond to the love of others.

Aphrodite Greek goddess of love, sexual ecstasy and beauty. Married by Zeus to Hephaestos, the smith god, in the hopes of controlling her wayward eye – an unsuccessful gambit. Hephaestos, adoring her, made her a magic girdle that rendered her yet more irresistible to males, both mortal and

deified. The priestesses at her temples were available for sex, regarded as an act of worship. Her festival was the Aphrodisiac; clearly she lent her name also to potions, etc., that promoted sexual desire.

Her Carian name was Aphrodisias, and this name was also given to the city in Asia Minor that became the centre of her cult.

Artemis (or **Amarynthia**, **Cynthia**) Greek goddess, the huntress, also a goddess of fertility and childbirth.

Asase Ya Ashanti goddess of the Earth and fertility, the mother of the trickster god Anansi.

Astarte (or **Ashtar**, **Ashtoreth**, **Athtar**, **Istar**) Phoenician goddess of reproduction and fertility, symbolizing the female principle; the Phoenician version of Ishtar. Astarte was the sister of Anat and the co-consort of Baal, who symbolized the male principle.

Astlik Armenian goddess of love, roughly equivalent to Aphrodite and Ishtar.

Atargatis Syrian fertility goddess, shown as half-fish, half-woman, and thus a contributor to the mermaid myth.

Ba Egyptian god of fertility and conception. He took the form of a ram.

Baal (or **Bel**) Phoenician, Babylonian, Canaanite and other cultures' god of fertility, of rain, of thunder and lightning, the Sun, and much else; he represented the male principle, the counterpart to Astarte's female principle. He died and was reborn each year; the ceremonies to mark this transition involved much sex as well as human sacrifices.

Bacchus Roman god of fertility and plenty, the equivalent of the Greek god Dionysos.

Benzai-ten (or **Benzai-tennyo**, **Benten**) Japanese eight-armed goddess of love and of the rich. Patron goddess of geishas, musicians and dancers.

Boann Irish fertility goddess, mother of Angus. Although married to Nechtan, she conceived Angus by the Dagda; to conceal this infidelity from Nechtan, she and the Dagda made the sun stand still for nine months, so Angus could be conceived and born all in a single day. She is totemized by a white cow.

Bona Dea (or **Fauna**) Roman fertility goddess whose worship was confined exclusively to women; the patron goddess of virginity and a goddess of medicine. She was totemized by serpents, in consciously phallic symbolism.

Branwen Celtic goddess of love and beauty, especially in Wales and the Isle of Man; she had attributes similar to those of Aphrodite. She died of a broken heart after the death of her brother Bran the Blessed.

Brigando (or **Brigandu**) Gallic goddess of fertility, arts and crafts. In Ireland her equivalent was called Brigid or Brigit; in Britain she was Brigantia. The Romans identified her with Minerva.

Ceres Roman goddess of fertility and maternal love, generally identified with the Greek Demeter.

Cernunnos (or **Herne**, **The Horned One**, **The Horned God**) Celtic god of fertility and much else, usually shown bearing the antlers of a stag. He was reborn each winter solstice and died each summer solstice. Rituals associated with him involved much sex and sometimes bloodshed.

Chac (or **Chac Mol**, **Ah Hoya**, **Hopop Caan**) Mayan fertility and agriculture god, controller of rain. Curiously for a fertility god, the rituals involved in entreating him to bring rain involved male sexual abstinence. One of his names, Ah Hoya, means "the urinator".

Chuang-Mu Chinese goddess of beds, the bedchamber, and events occurring in the latter.

Cupid Roman god of love and desire, the messenger of Venus. He was a small winged boy who fired arrows at the hearts of unsuspecting mortals to make them fall in love; the equivalent of the Greek Eros.

Venus, outraged by the beauty of the mortal woman Psyche, sent Cupid to cause her to fall in love with the ugliest man in the world. However, Cupid himself fell in love with Psyche – and she with him, even though he insisted she keep her chamber dark so she could not see him. One night Psyche, irresistibly curious, lit a lamp while Cupid slept so she might see her lover; however, a drop of hot oil she spilled wakened him. Enraged by her deception, he left her. Anguished, Psyche roamed the world in search of him until Jove took pity on her and reunited them.

Cybele (or **Kybele**, **Earth Mother**, **The Great Mother**, **The Goddess**) Perhaps the most important and influential deity in human history, the goddess of nature, fertility and much else, worshipped in various guises in numerous cultures. Her milder Greek form was Rhea. Cybele was perhaps originally from Phrygia. In the Roman culture her castrated priests were the Corybantes. Ceremonies associated with her were orgiastic and often murderous. Her Celtic form was far more beneficent, but if anything more powerful.

Dagan (or **Dagon**) God of fertility and agriculture worshipped over a wide area of the Near East. He was the father of Baal (or Bel), who eventually supplanted him.

Dambala Important Voodoo god, the father of the loa, and a fertility god.

Demeter Greek fertility goddess who taught humankind agriculture. She was mother of Persephone, who was abducted by Hades to the underworld as his bride. Demeter was so distraught by the loss of her daughter that no crops grew. Eventually Zeus ordered Hades to return Persephone, but through Hades's trickery Persephone is still bound to the underworld for three months of the year, during which time Demeter, missing her, shirks her duties of helping crops to grow.

Diana Roman goddess, the huntress, equivalent of the Greek Artemis. A goddess of fertility and childbirth.

Dionysos The twice-born: Greek god of fertility, wine and plenty. He seems to have been a combination of a relatively benign Greek nature god and a more savage god later adopted from Phrygia.

Enki Sumerian Lord of the Abyss, wisdom and semen, and god of fertility, water and creation.

Eros Greek god of love and desire, later adapted by the Romans to be their god Cupid. The mythology is unclear as to whether he was a relatively late god (the son of Aphrodite and Ares) or one of the primeval ones, responsible for bringing humankind into existence. He is usually shown as a winged boy armed with bow and arrows, which latter he shoots at people's hearts: gold-tipped arrows whose flights were made of dove feathers engendered love in the recipient; lead-tipped arrows with flights made of owl feathers engendered indifference.

Fortuna Roman goddess of fertility and good fortune, a goddess especially of mothers.

Freya Norse goddess of love, sexuality and fertility. On death, women went to Freya's hall at Folkvang, as did half the warriors slain in battle, the other half going to Odin's hall. She was married to the god Od (an aspect of Odin), took the human lover Ottar (shown with her in disguise as the boar Hildesvini), and gained the famed Necklace of the Brisings through sleeping with four dwarfs. She was of great beauty.

Frigga Norse goddess of love, fertility, marriage and mother-hood; the wife of Odin. She and Freya are often confused, and may have been different aspects of each other.

Gefion Norse fertility goddess, possibly an aspect of Frigga, and the patron goddess of virgins; all women who died virgins became her servants.

Hathor Egyptian goddess of love, tombs and the sky. A daughter of Ra and depicted as a woman with cows' horns, she mothered the world (including the Sun), and each evening welcomed the Sun back to her bosom. The Pharaohs were said to be wetnursed by her, and through her milk be elevated to godhood. When Ra decided humankind should be exterminated, it was Hathor he enlisted to conduct the slaughter; she did this with such zeal that an appalled Ra tricked her into getting so drunk she couldn't continue.

Hebat Hittite goddess of beauty and fertility, an equivalent of

Astarte and Ishtar. Her consort, the fertility god Teshub, died and was reborn each year.

Heqet Egyptian goddess of childbirth, shown as a frog or as a frog-headed woman.

Hera Greek goddess, the Queen of the Gods, wife of Zeus and goddess of marriage and childbirth. Much of Greek mythology stems from Hera's fury over Zeus's promiscuity. She was able to restore her own virginity each year by bathing in a well called Canathus.

Idun Norse goddess of youth and fertility. She guarded the golden apples the gods ate to regain their youth whenever they approached old age.

Inanna (or **Inannu**) Sumerian goddess of love, fertility and war, associated with the sky and the planet Venus. The most important of all the Sumerian goddesses, she was a cruel flirt who led men on and then dumped them at the last moment.

Ishtar Babylonian and Sumerian goddess of love, procreation and war, an equivalent of Aphrodite but far crueler: she had the habit of destroying her lovers. In the Epic of Gilgamesh she tries to marry the hero but is rejected because of past cruelties. She seeks vengeance from her father Anu, god of the air, who gives her a bull to set upon Gilgamesh. However, Gilgamesh beheads the bull and casts its body at her feet. She avenges herself by killing Gilgamesh's companion Enkidu.

Isis Egyptian goddess of motherhood and womanhood, among much else. Daughter of the Earth and Sky, she was sister and wife to Osiris, and acted as regent during his many absences. After Osiris's murder by Set, she was able to revive the dead body long enough to impregnate herself, bearing Horus. Set then vengefully dismembered Osiris's corpse, but even this wasn't enough to deter the dogged widow, who assembled the pieces (all except the penis, which had been eaten by a crocodile), embalmed the result, and thereby brought Osiris immortality. He retired to the underworld, leaving Isis in charge.

Kama Hindu god, described in some early versions of the Vedas as the supreme Creator but later regarded primarily as the god of sexual desire. He had a bow with which he shot flower-tipped arrows to kindle love and sexual passions in mortals and gods alike. In one myth he shot Shiva, who furiously killed him; for a long time there was neither love nor sexual desire in the world, which accordingly became a desert. At last Shiva was prevailed upon by the other gods to let Kama be reborn as Pradyumna, and matters were set aright.

Khem Egyptian god of fertility, reproduction and agriculture, a precursor of the Greek god Pan.

Kurukulla Tibetan goddess of love who habitually captivates men and gods alike. Often shown sitting atop the love god Kama.

Lakshmi Hindu goddess, mother of the love god Kama and herself the goddess of beauty and good fortune. Like Aphrodite, she was born from sea foam.

Lupercus Roman fertility god, generally depicted as half-naked, the other half being clad in goatskin.

Marduk (or **Bel**) Mesopotamian fertility god, destroyer of the dragons of chaos, creator of the universe and human life, and much else besides.

Min Egyptian god of fertility and male sexuality, sometimes identified with Horus, sometimes with the Greek god Pan. Min was frequently shown clutching his own doughty erection in his left hand so there could be no mistaking his affinities.

The Morrigan Irish tripartite fertility goddess, also goddess of war, strife and sexual ecstasy. She has equivalents in many other mythologies, notably the Norse Valkyries, and has connections to the legends of Morgan le Fay.

♡

Nantosuelta Celtic (Gallic) fertility goddess, goddess of nature, streams and valleys, and a goddess of the underworld.

Nawang Wulan Javanese goddess of love and fertility; the goddess of the Moon.

Ningizzida (or **Gizzida**) Mesopotamian fertility god, often shown with the head of a man and the body of a serpent.

♡

Oshun Yoruba goddess of love, sensuality and creativity. Usually benign, but vicious when provoked.

Ostara Anglo-Saxon fertility goddess of the rising sun and Spring. In one myth she made a rabbit lay coloured eggs, which she gave to children; hence Easter eggs, the Easter Bunny and indeed, from "Ostara", the name "Easter" itself.

♡

Pan Greek god of male desire and sexuality. Shown as a pipe-playing satyr or as a goat. His favoured occupation was chasing mortal and immortal women.

Pan Jin Lian Chinese goddess of fornication, the patron goddess of prostitutes.

Papa Maori Earth goddess. She fell in love with the sky god, Rangi, and the two made love without cease and with such vigour that the plants of the world stopped growing. At last the other gods prised them apart and things returned to normal.

Prende Illyrian goddess of love and (curiously) also a saint of the Catholic Church.

Priapus (or **Ithyphallus**, **Tychon**) Roman and pre-Roman fertility god, famed for his constantly exposed erection. Statues of him, rampant, were placed in gardens to encourage fertility and act as a scarecrow.

Qadesh Syrian goddess of love and sexual bliss. She was later imported into Egypt as Qetesh.

Renenutet (or **Renenet**, **Ernutet**) Egyptian fertility goddess, shown as a cobra or with a cobra's head.

Rosmerta Celtic (Gaulish) fertility goddess, also the goddess of fire and plenty.

Saule Latvian goddess identified with the Sun and thus a goddess of fertility. In her aspects of mother and lover, she was the patron goddess of orphans and other unfortunates.

Selene Greek goddess of the Moon, and hence of romance; the sister of the Sun god Helios. Of her many romantic liaisons, the best known is that with the mortal Endymion.

Shabbat Hamalka Judaic goddess of the Sabbath, a female aspect of – and, in her guise as Shekhina, bride of – Yahweh's male aspect, Yesod. As Queen of the Shabbat, and personification of the Shabbat, she became much associated with sex and romance; it became the holy obligation of spouses to make love at midnight on Fridays, reflecting similar lovemaking at that time between Shekhina and Yesod.

Shakti Hindu goddess, the female principle, the creative power within us, represented as the female genitalia and capable of incarnating herself as a male's sexual partner. Alternatively she could dwell in the seventh heaven, where mystics might make love with her during their transcendental travels. At the moment of death a man made love with Shakti for the last time.

Sheila–na–gig Celtic fertility goddess, whose overt sexuality acted as a counter to death.

Silvanus Roman fertility god, the god of forests and wild places; a diluted version of the Greek god Pan.

Sopdet Egyptian fertility goddess, the personification of the star Sirius. Adopted by the Greeks as Sothis, she later became just an aspect of Isis.

Suadela Roman goddess, an adherent of Venus. Her responsibility was persuasion and in particular seduction.

Teutates (or **Albiorix**, **Caturix**, **Loucetius**, **Rigisamos**) Celtic god of fertility, war and plenty.

Tlazolteotl Aztec goddess of sex and childbirth, among her duties as Earth Mother. She was also a sin-eater, appearing at the time of death to eat all a person's evils.

Uliliyassis Hittite god in charge of curing erectile dysfunction.

Umay (or **Ayisit**) Turkic goddess of fertility and childbirth, especially involved in human activities during birth and the first few days of life.

Uni Etruscan goddess of love and marriage. She bore to the sky god Tin a son called Hercle, or Hercules.

Venus Roman goddess of love, beauty and sexuality, the equivalent of the Greek goddess Aphrodite. She had many lovers among the gods and even among mortals; nonetheless, the Caesars, who claimed descent from her via her son Aeneas (fathered by a mortal, Anchises), worshipped her in the form of Venus Genetrix, goddess of marriage and maternity. Her most famous liaison, immortalized by Shakespeare among many other writers and artists, was with the mortal "heavenly youth" Adonis.

Xochiquetzal Aztec goddess of love with special responsibility for pregnancy, childbirth and prostitution.

Zemepatis (or **Dimstipatis**, **Zemininkas**) Lithuanian fertility god, patron god of the family home. Brother of Zemyna, the Earth goddess.

OTHER LOVE DEITIES
WORTH A TRY

Alalahe/Alilmenehune Oceanian goddess of love.

Allat/Allatu Pre-Islamic Arab fertility goddess.

Andarta Gallic goddess of fertility.

Antheia Cretan goddess of fertility and love.

Asherah/Asherat Syrian fertility goddess.

Astrild Norse goddess of love.

Bat/Bata Egyptian fertility goddess, taking the form of a cow.

Bhumidevi Hindu fertility goddess, second wife of Vishnu.

Bres Irish fertility god, husband of the goddess Brigid.

Curche Prussian god of fertility, akin to Dionysos.

Faunus Roman god of fertility and agriculture.

Haumea Polynesian goddess of fertility and childbirth.

Hnoss Norse goddess of sensuality and infatuation.

Huixtocihuatl/Uixtochihuatl Aztec fertility goddess.

Hyacinthus Greek god of male love.

Kapo Hawaiian fertility goddess.

Kotharat Canaanite god of conception and childbirth.

Liber Early Roman fertility god, later conflated with Dionysos.

Libera Female counterpart and consort of Liber.

Lofn Norse goddess of adultery and other illicit liaisons.

Mabon Welsh god of love.

Mama Allpa Many-breasted Incan fertility goddess.

Musubi-no-Kami Japanese god of love and marriage.

Mylitta Assyrian and Babylonian goddess of birth and fertility.

Nanaja Sumerian goddess of sexuality and war.

Ngendi Fijian fertility god who taught humankind how to use fire.

Niu-Lang Minor Chinese god of love.

Rati Hindu goddess of carnal desire; the wife of Kama.

Sarasvati Hindu goddess of fertility, learning, writing, rivers and much else.

Sita Hindu goddess, the female principle and the wife of Rama.

Sjofn Norse goddess of love, sexuality and harmony.

Sucellus Gallic god of fertility and abundance.

Turan Etruscan equivalent of Venus.

Ueuecoyotl Aztec coyote god of frivolity and sex.

Ukemochi Shinto goddess of fertility and eating.

Urvasi Hindu patron goddess of success in love.

Volupta/Voluptua Greek and Roman goddess of sensual pleasure.

Wawalag/Wawalug Twin-sister Australian Aboriginal fertility goddesses.

Xochipili Aztec god of love and pleasantness.

Xochipili

WRITERS OF ROMANCE

A romance novel can be defined as one that focuses on the initiation and development of a romantic relationship between a man and a woman that is expected to last happily ever after.

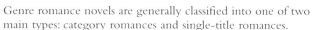

Genre romance novels are generally classified into one of two main types: category romances and single-title romances.

Category romances are those published as part of a series of similar romances issued by the same publisher. They are usually of standard (fairly short) length, and, much like magazines, are expected to have a limited shelf-life, being replaced within a few weeks by the next batch of romances issued in that line by the same publisher.

The publication of single-title romances is more like that of any other novel. They are not usually expected to be uniform in length or style, although their content *is* expected to be in accordance with the rules outlined above. Confusingly, many single-title romances fall into series of books featuring the same or a similar cast of characters and written by the same author.

There are numerous subgenres of the romance novel. A partial list would include: contemporary, historical, paranormal, fantasy, sciencefictional, suspense, Western, timeslip, inspirational and erotic – erotic romances are often called "romantica" to distinguish them from mainstream erotica (or simply so that their readers will be less embarrassed about buying them).

Most of these subgenres have further subdivisions; for example, a very high percentage of historical romances fall into the Regency sub-subgenre. Crossovers between subgenres are common – historical suspense, for example – as are crossovers with other genres: many novels published as genre fantasies are also romances, and so on.

The premier association of romantic writers in the USA is Romance Writers of America, Inc. (RWA), founded in 1980 and currently with some 9000 members. Its counterpart in Britain is the Romantic Novelists' Association (RNA), founded in 1960, with about 700 members (of whom some 20 are male).

Awards are sponsored by both organizations. The RWA's main awards include the RWA Lifetime Achievement Award, the Golden Heart Award, and the Rita (named for the association's first president, Rita Clay Estrada). The RNA sponsors the Foster Grant Romantic Novel of the Year Award, the RNA Romance Award and the Joan Hessayon New Writers' Award, as well as the Elizabeth Goudge Trophy.

In the USA, according to the most recent (2003) figures released by the RWA, romantic novels made up 48.8% of mass-market paperback sales, and were read by over 50 million people annually. In that year, 2093 new titles were released by US publishers, and sales totalled $1.41 billion.

Even more tellingly, in 2003 an astonishing 33.8% of *all* fiction sales were of romantic novels. By way of comparison, science fiction accounted for 6.0% and mystery 25.6%.

Among readers of romantic fiction, 2% read over 100 new romance titles per year.

Surveyed in 2002, according to the RWA, readers of romantic fiction listed muscularity as the most desirable characteristic in a hero, followed by (in order) handsomeness and

intelligence. The top three most desirable characteristics in a heroine were (again in order) intelligence, strength of character, and attractiveness.

Almost certainly the most prolific romantic novelist of all time has been Barbara Cartland. Born Mary Barbara Hamilton Cartland in 1901 in Edgbaston, England, by the time of her death in 2000 she had published 723 books (an average of two per month) under several names aside from her own, and racked up worldwide sales reportedly in excess of one billion copies. She also left the manuscripts of 130 unpublished novels; these began to be published from 2004. She in fact dictated rather than wrote her novels, with transcription by secretaries. She was stepmother to Raine, Countess Spencer, who was herself stepmother to Diana, Princess of Wales.

The most prolific current practitioner of romantic fiction is the US writer Nora Roberts, who also publishes as J.D. Robb. By the end of 2004 there were reported to be over 280 million copies of her books in print, with sales averaging 23 per minute. She began publishing in 1981 with *Irish Thoroughbred*, the sixth novel she had written, and by 2004 had published over 120 novels under the two names. In that year she was the ninth highest earner on Forbes List, with an annual income estimated at $60 million.

Another prolific romance writer was Eleanor Alice Burford Hibbert, who wrote as Victoria Holt, Philippa Carr and Jean Plaidy. Born in London in 1906, she published her first novel, *Beyond the Blue Mountains*, as Plaidy, in 1948; 82 further Plaidy novels followed, plus two children's books and five nonfictions. The first of her 32 Victoria Holt books, *Mistress of Mellyn*, was published in 1960. The first of her 20 Philippa Carr books (one posthumous) was *The Miracle at St Bruno's* (1972).

The British novelist Louise de la Ramée (1839–1908), who wrote as Ouida, produced over 40 romantic novels, most of them dashing adventures. Best known are probably *Under Two Flags* (1867) and *A Dog of Flanders* (1872). Her pseudonym was derived from her attempts as a baby to pronounce her own name, Louise.

Although more generally regarded as a social satirist, Jane Austen (1775–1817) has her place in the pantheon of romantic novelists. Of her six major novels, four were published during the last few years of her life and two appeared posthumously: *Sense and Sensibility* (1811), *Pride and Prejudice* (1813), *Mansfield Park* (1814), *Emma* (1815), *Northanger Abbey* (1818), and *Persuasion* (1818). Written in 1795 but unpublished during her lifetime was the short novel *Lady Susan*; unfinished novels were *The Watsons* and *Sanditon*. Several "completions" of these latter two have been published.

The three Brontë sisters Charlotte (1816–1855), Emily (1818–1848) and Anne (1820–1849) between them set the stage for the development of the modern romantic novel. All died young; by the time Charlotte died, having not yet reached the age of 40, she had been preceded by two older sisters who died in childhood, by Emily and Anne, and by their only brother, Patrick Branwell (1817–1848).

Charlotte's novels were *Jane Eyre* (1847), *Shirley* (1849), *Villette* (1853) and the posthumous *The Professor* (1857); the latter two were inspired by her attraction to M. Constantin Heger, who ran the Brussels *pensionnat* where she taught for two periods during 1842–44. Emily's single novel, *Wuthering Heights* (1847), may well be the best-selling romantic novel of all time; it has been adapted for the screen several times and in 1978 was even "adapted" as a hit rock single by songwriter Kate Bush (covered in the USA by Pat Benatar in 1980); curiously, Bush and Emily Brontë share the same birthday, July 30.

Anne's two novels were *Agnes Grey* (1846) and *The Tenant of Wildfell Hall* (1847), the latter's dissolute central character being supposedly based on brother Branwell.

Sister to actress Joan Collins, romantic novelist Jackie Collins is less prolific than some of her rivals, with a "mere" 20 or so novels to date, but her worldwide sales of a claimed 400 million books put her novels of sex, crime and Hollywood razzmatazz well up the list of bestsellers. Sister Joan starred in the first two movies based on Jackie's novels, *The Stud* (1978) and *The Bitch* (1979).

British-born US romantic novelist Barbara Taylor Bradford's first published novel was *A Woman of Substance* (1979), and it had been followed by 19 others by the end of 2004; she has in addition written nonfiction and children's books. By then she had sold an estimated 75 million books worldwide. Ten of her novels have been adapted for the screen as television movies or miniseries with phenomenal success; all of these have been produced by her husband Robert.

The British romantic novelist Catherine Cookson (1906–1998), who wrote also as Catherine Marchant and Katie McMullen (her maiden name), was author of 88 romantic/historical novels as well as some books for children and three volumes of autobiography. Her sales exceeded 100 million. She created the Catherine Cookson Foundation in 1985, and through it made donations of extraordinary generosity. In the last decade or more of her life her novels started to become accepted as significant by the mainstream literary establishment. She became Dame Catherine Cookson in 1993. Her husband Tom, a teacher whom she married in 1943, survived her by just three weeks; he had from early on transcribed and edited all her books.

Another prolific writer, Georgette Heyer (1902–1974), did not invent but seems almost to define the romantic-historical subgenre. About a dozen of her 60 or so novels were mysteries in the Agatha Christie vein; most of the remainder were Regency romances.

One of the biggest hitters among current romantic novelists is Danielle Steel, author of 65 books (to March 2005) with worldwide sales reported at 530 million. Of these books, an astonishing 24 have been made into television movies. Not a novel is *His Bright Light* (1998), an account of the life of her son Nick, a manic depressive who committed suicide at age 19. She has become active in causes related to mental illness and bipolar disorder.

US romantic novelist Kathleen Winsor (1919–2003) wrote only six books, but the first of these, the historical romance *Forever Amber* (1944), scandalized the nation, was widely condemned as pornography, and was banned in various regions, including Boston; it was filmed by Otto Preminger in 1947. Thanks in large part to the controversy, the book sold over a million copies in its first year. Winsor later recalled that there were only two really sexy passages in the manuscript, both of which were excised by her publisher and replaced by ellipses.

Notoriety surrounded the career of British romantic novelist Elinor Glyn (1864–1943), author of 25 novels. Curiously, she turned to writing through distaste for the superficiality and moral laxity of the Victorian aristocracy into which she had been introduced through her friendship with the mistress of the Prince of Wales. Her early novels were romantic social satires in the Jane Austen mould, but in *Three Weeks* (1907) she told the erotic tale of the brief romance between a young Englishman and a mysterious older woman who proves to be a Balkan queen and who famously seduces him on a tiger-skin rug within a mere three days of their first meeting. Widely censured as pornographic, the book promptly sold by the million.

　　　Glyn's later life reads like one of her racier novels. She was the adulterous lover of Lord Curzon for eight years; the affair ended when she read in her daily newspaper of his engagement. She moved in 1920 to Hollywood, where she wrote several screenplays – including that for *Three Weeks* (1924) – and coined the term "It". Published in book form and also filmed in 1927, the short novel *It* rekindled the notoriety Glyn had attracted with *Three Weeks*.

The Gothic romance could be said to have been invented by Hugh Walpole (1717–1797) with *The Castle of Otranto: A*

Gothic Story (1764). In its first edition Walpole claimed it was a translation from an Italian original, but later he admitted the supposed Italian novel did not exist.

The British novelist Ann Radcliffe (1764–1823) can be regarded as the grandmother of the hugely popular Gothic romance subgenre. Of her eight novels, six were published during her lifetime. Her best-known work is *The Mysteries of Udolpho* (1794), closely followed by *The Italian* (1797). Jane Austen's *Northanger Abbey* (1818) is a pleasing parody of the Radcliffe oeuvre.

The bestselling romantic novel of all time may well be Erich Segal's *Love Story*. Originally Segal wrote this as a movie script, but his agent, Lois Wallace, made him turn the script into a novel. This was serialized in *Ladies' Home Journal* in February 1970. Harper & Row published the book soon after in hardback with a first print run of 57,000; there were 430,000 copies of the hardback in print by the end of the year. In November 1970 the mass-market paperback was released with a first print run of 4,350,000 copies, with a further 600,000 printing ordered the following day. Unusually for the USA, the paperback release did not kill the hardback: a month later, the hardback was still selling at the rate of 2000 copies per week. Total sales figures to date are not known, but by the end of 1987 the estimate was 21 million.

The movie itself broke records, earning $321,688 within its first two weeks – a paltry sum by today's standards, but unprecedented then. It was nominated for seven Academy Awards, but won just one (musical score).

Soon after the book's publication, Yale, where Segal was a professor of classics and comparative literature, denied him tenure.

THE STATISTICS OF LOVE

Love and romance are not susceptible to scientific analysis, and neither can they be reduced to a matter of numbers. However, the behaviour of people in love can be numerically analysed. While every romance – like every pair of lovers – is of course unique, statistics show us how our behaviours conform to large-scale patterns.

Among people in their 20s in the USA, there are about six single women for every five single men. For the over-65s, however, there are about three women who have never married for every one man who has never married.

54% of US women over 15 and 57% of US men over 15 are married. In 2000 in the UK, 47.5% of the population were married.

In the UK the average age of the partners at first marriage has been gently rising over the past few decades:

In 1851 (no 1850 figures available) the median first-time groom was aged 24.38 years, his bride 23.38 years;

By 1900, grooms were likely to be 25.37 years old and brides 23.95;

By 1950, the figures were relatively unchanged at 25.32 and 22.73 respectively;

LIVING TOGETHER

In 2003, 4.2% of all US households were maintained by cohabiting rather than married couples. This figure appears to be gently rising as time goes on, up from 0.8% in 1960 and 1970, 2.0% in 1980, and 3.1% in 1990.

Perhaps a more telling figure is that in the US about 65% of all married couples cohabited beforehand.In the UK, however, cohabitation has become commonplace. A 2002 survey showed that about one-quarter of all unmarried adults were living in a cohabitation, with highs in the country's Southeast and Southwest regions (29% and 31% respectively) and lows in Scotland and Northern Ireland (both 20%). A somewhat older survey (1993) showed that the highest cohabitation rates of all were among divorced men, over 40% of whom were cohabiting.

A 2003 UK survey of cohabitation concluded that on average a first-time cohabitation whose partners in the end decided not to marry lasted 36 months, and a similar second-time cohabitation slightly less long, at 32 months.

The rate at which premarital cohabitation is becoming the norm in the UK is revealed by surveys done of women in the mid-1960s and the early 1990s. In the earlier survey, only about 5% of single women lived with their future husbands before marriage; by 1994 this figure had risen to 70%. Most strikingly, for women who had been previously married to someone else the figure was approximately 90%.

However, cohabitation may not be a good idea as a trial for marriage. UK Government statistics from 1992 revealed that 39% of marriages that had been preceded by cohabitation ended in divorce, compared with 21% of those that had not.

Because of persisting social pressures or for other reasons, women seem much less happy with the cohabitation lifestyle than men are. A 1995 UK survey showed that, while 15% of married women had been treated for neurotic illness over the survey period, the figure for cohabiting women was 24%. The (much lower) percentage for men showed  no difference between the two lifestyles.

Similarly for anxiety and depressive disorders: 13.3% of cohabiting women suffered these, compared with 8.6% of married women. For men, too, there was a difference, albeit much smaller: the relevant figures were 6.4% and 5.1%.

One reason for the stark difference between the mental health of cohabiting and married women might be that the former are very likely to be subject to a constant barrage of criticism over the situation from elderly relatives, commonly in the belief that they're acting "for her own good".

By 1975, the median ages had actually decreased a little: 23.63 years and 21.42 years;

By 1990, those figures were climbing significantly from their 1975 levels: 26.14 and 24.26;

And by 2002 (the most recent year for which figures have been published) the median ages were 30.1 years for first-time grooms and 27.9 years for first-time brides.

Approximately one-third of all children born in the USA are born out of wedlock. The parallel figure for the UK is quite a lot lower, being 25.7% in 2003.

♡

About 21% of US husbands commit adultery at some stage during the marriage; the figure for wives is about 13.5%.

♡

According to a 2001 United Nations report, the USA is the country with the highest annual per capita rate of marriage. The Top Ten countries, with their rates given as the number of marriages per 1000 members of the population, are:

USA	9.8	Israel	7.0
Russia	8.9	New Zealand	7.0
Czech Republic	8.4	Australia	6.9
Romania	8.3	Switzerland	6.9
Portugal	7.3	UK	6.8

♡

On average, about 6000 couples get married each day in the USA.

♡

The other side of marriage is of course divorce. Here is a comparable Top Ten for divorce rates (per 1000 of the population):

USA	4.95	New Zealand	2.63
Puerto Rico	4.47	Australia	2.52
Russia	3.36	Canada	2.46
UK	3.08	Finland	1.85
Denmark	2.81	Barbados	1.21

♡

On average, about 3000 couples get divorced each day in the USA; i.e., 50% of the number getting married.

Church marriages are steadily losing out to civil ceremonies, at least in the UK. In 1981, about 51% of all British marriages were solemnized at a religious ceremony as opposed to a civil one. By 1991 this figure was essentially unchanged, at 50.6%. All through the 1990s the percentage declined, and by 2002, with marriage figures as a whole having dropped sharply, only about 34% of all marriages had the benefit of a religious ceremony.

Approximately 80% of all engagement rings in the West contain one or more diamonds.

Although it is commonly stated that about 10% of any human population is gay, surveys do not bear this out. It is almost impossible to estimate how many of either sex are practising heterosexuals while covertly homosexuals, but surveys of people's past sexual encounters indicate that about 6% of men over 18 (to exclude adolescent experiments) are either exclusively gay or bisexual, about half of the total being bisexual. The figures for women over 18 are less easily obtained, but it seems they are about one-third lower in total, with nearly 80% of gay/bisexual women being bisexual.

Contrary to popular outcries about rising sexual activity among the young, statistical surveys in the USA show if anything a gentle decline in recent years. Among male high-school students surveyed in 1990, 60.8% were no longer virgins; in 1997 this figure had dropped to 48.8%. Among women the figures had stayed roughly the same, 48.0% and 47.7% respectively. The story is rather different if one looks at a longer timescale. Although figures for men are not readily available, surveys of US women aged 15–19 show that in 1970 71% were still virgins, while in 1995 that figure had dropped to 50% (having been as low as 45% in the interim).

According to a 1995 survey of US high school students, the median age at which sexually experienced young men first made love was 16.4 years, with the equivalent for women being a statistically insignificant month or so higher, at 16.5 years. This makes rather a nonsense of the legal age of consent being 18 in much of the USA.

The summer is the time to be married, and January by far the least popular month of all – or, at least, that's what people seem to think. Here are the 2002 figures for the UK (those months indicated ★ contained five Saturdays that year rather than four, so affecting the figures upward):

January	6,788	July	31,097
February	10,850	August	43,957★
March	14,255★	September	30,617
April	15,105	October	18,806
May	24,385	November	14,283★
June	31,634★	December	13,819

On average, US adults make love about 60 times per year. For married couples the figures are higher, as might be expected: about 66 times per year. Less anticipated might be that adults who have been married but are now separated achieve a higher average than this, 69 times per year, and adults who have remarried average a whopping 74 times per year! For married couples in the 18–29 age-bracket, the figure is 111.6 times per year.